Color Me
WILD

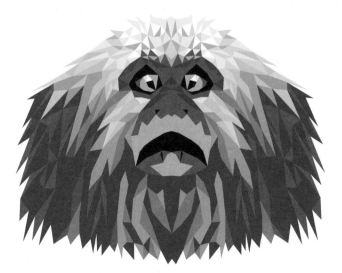

Trianimals: Color Me Wild
Copyright © 2016 by RotoVision

Published in 2016 by:
Harper Design
An Imprint of HarperCollinsPublishers
195 Broadway
New York, NY 10007
Tel: (212) 207-7000
Fax: (855) 746-6023
harperdesign@harpercollins.com
www.hc.com

Distributed throughout North America by
HarperCollinsPublishers
195 Broadway
New York, NY 10007

ISBN 978-0-06-248451-2

Printed in China

First Printing, 2016

Publisher: Mark Searle
Editorial Director: Isheeta Mustafi
Commissioning Editor: Alison Morris
Junior Editor: Abbie Sharman
Editor: Joanne Reeder
Cover design: Michelle Rowlandson
Layout: Michelle Rowlandson and Agata Rybicka

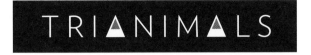

TRIANIMALS

Color Me
WILD

60 Color-by-Number
Geometric Artworks with Bite

HOPE LITTLE & ÇETIN CAN KARADUMAN

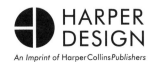

HARPER
DESIGN

An Imprint of HarperCollins Publishers

Welcome to
TRIANIMALS

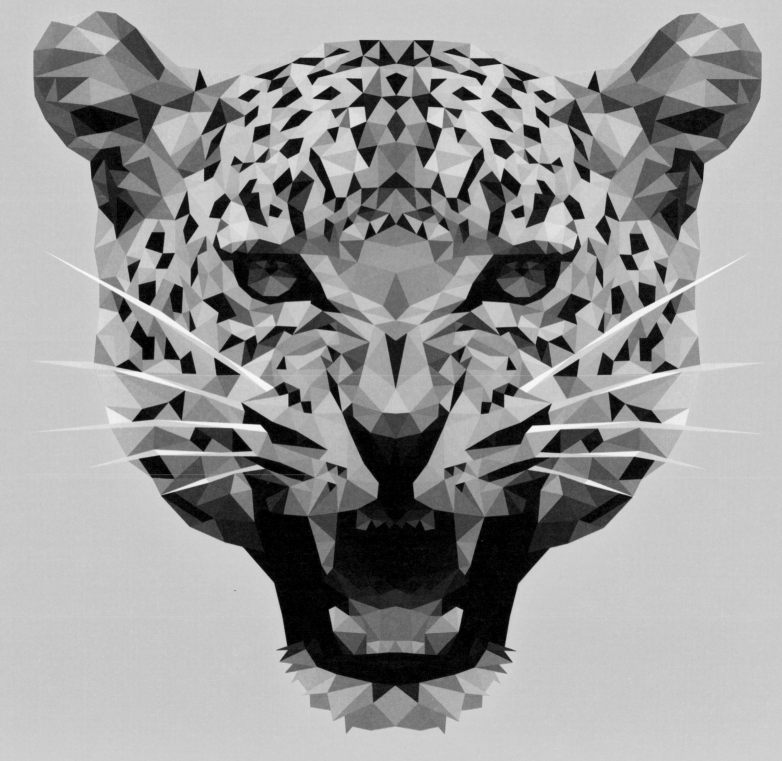

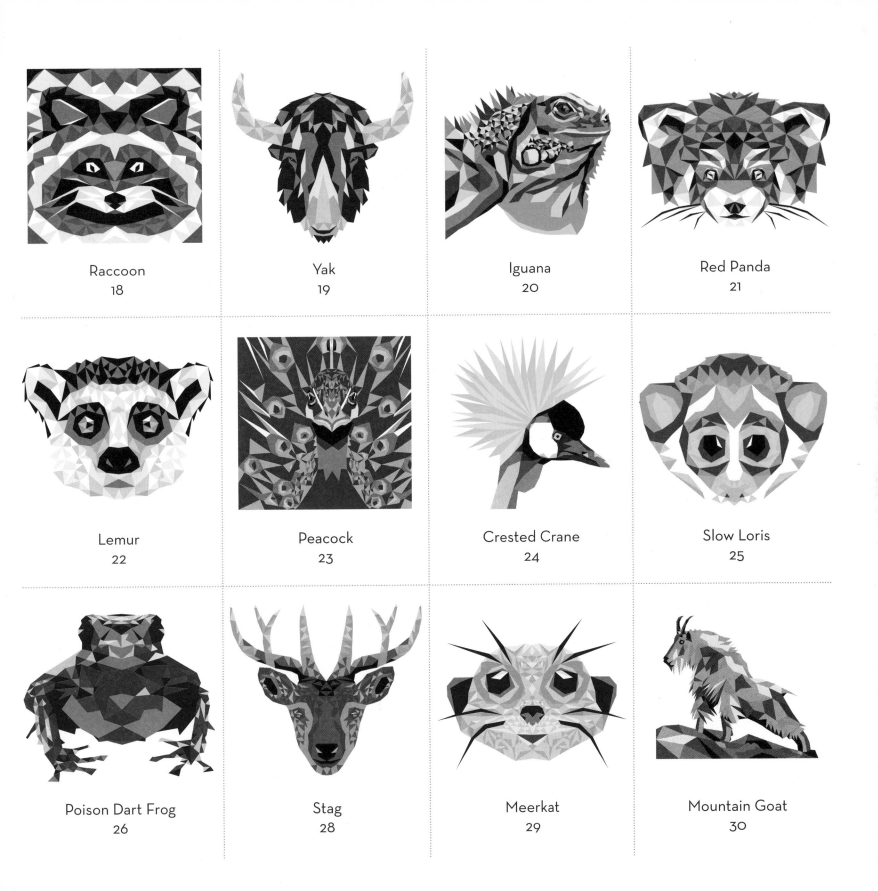

Raccoon
18

Yak
19

Iguana
20

Red Panda
21

Lemur
22

Peacock
23

Crested Crane
24

Slow Loris
25

Poison Dart Frog
26

Stag
28

Meerkat
29

Mountain Goat
30

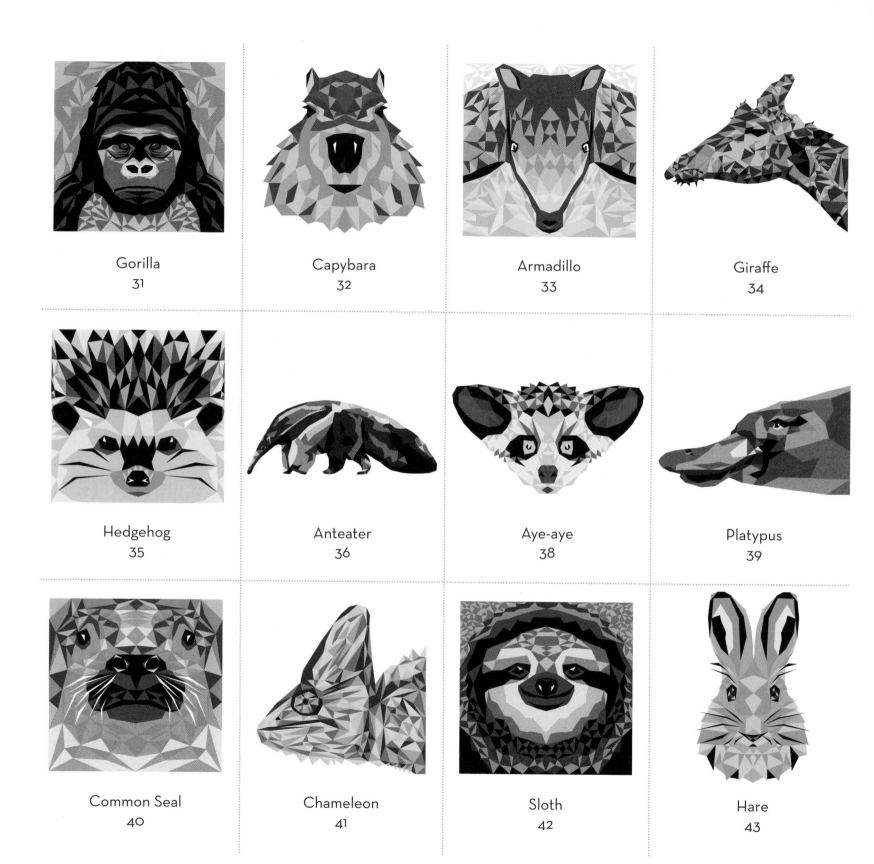

Gorilla
31

Capybara
32

Armadillo
33

Giraffe
34

Hedgehog
35

Anteater
36

Aye-aye
38

Platypus
39

Common Seal
40

Chameleon
41

Sloth
42

Hare
43

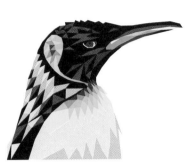

Penguin
44

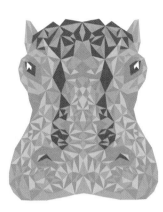

Hippopotamus
45

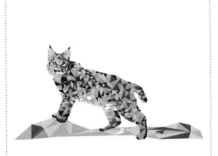

Bobcat
46

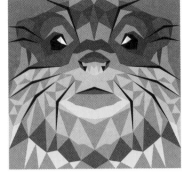

Otter
48

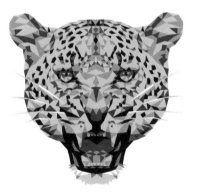

Cheetah
49

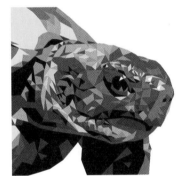

Tortoise
50

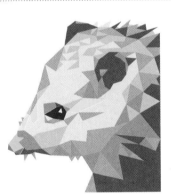

Opossum
51

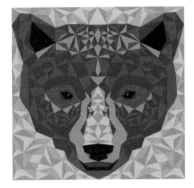

Brown Bear
52

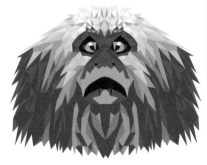

Golden Lion Tamarin
53

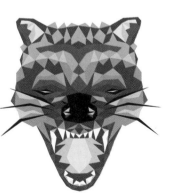

Hyena
54

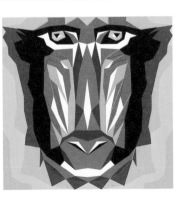

Mandrill
55

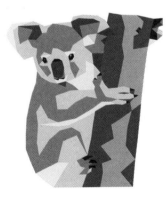

Koala
56

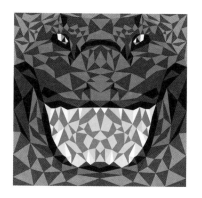

Alligator
58

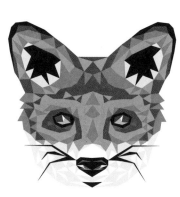

Fox
59

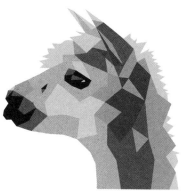

Llama
60

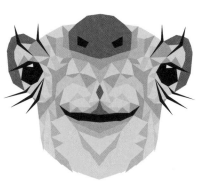

Camel
61

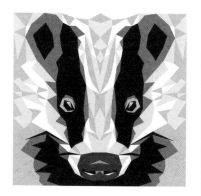

Badger
62

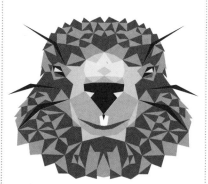

Beaver
63

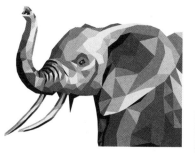

Elephant
64

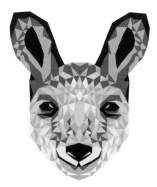

Kangaroo
65

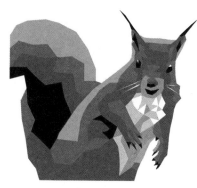

Red Squirrel
66

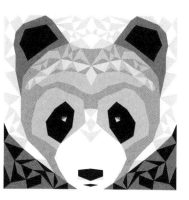

Panda
68

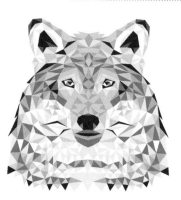

Wolf
69

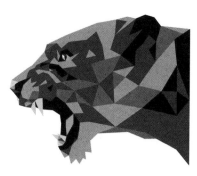

Lioness
70

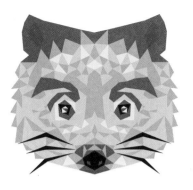

Wombat
71

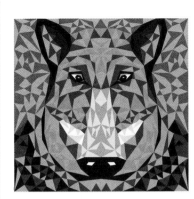

Wild Boar
72

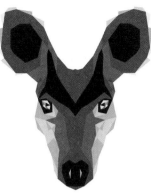

Okapi
73

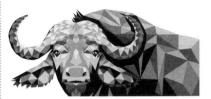

Cape Buffalo
74

MASKS

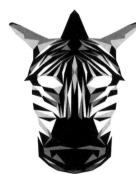

Zebra
81

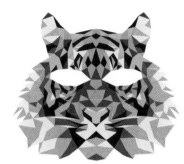

Orangutan
83

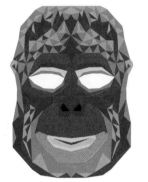

Tiger
85

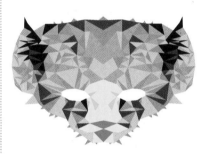

Vampire Bat
87

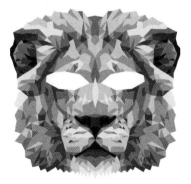

Lion
89

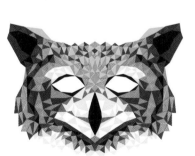

Great Horned Owl
91

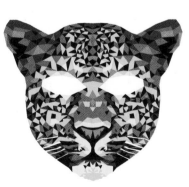

Leopard
93

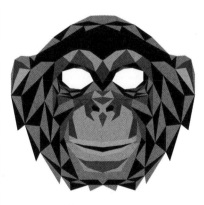

Chimpanzee
95

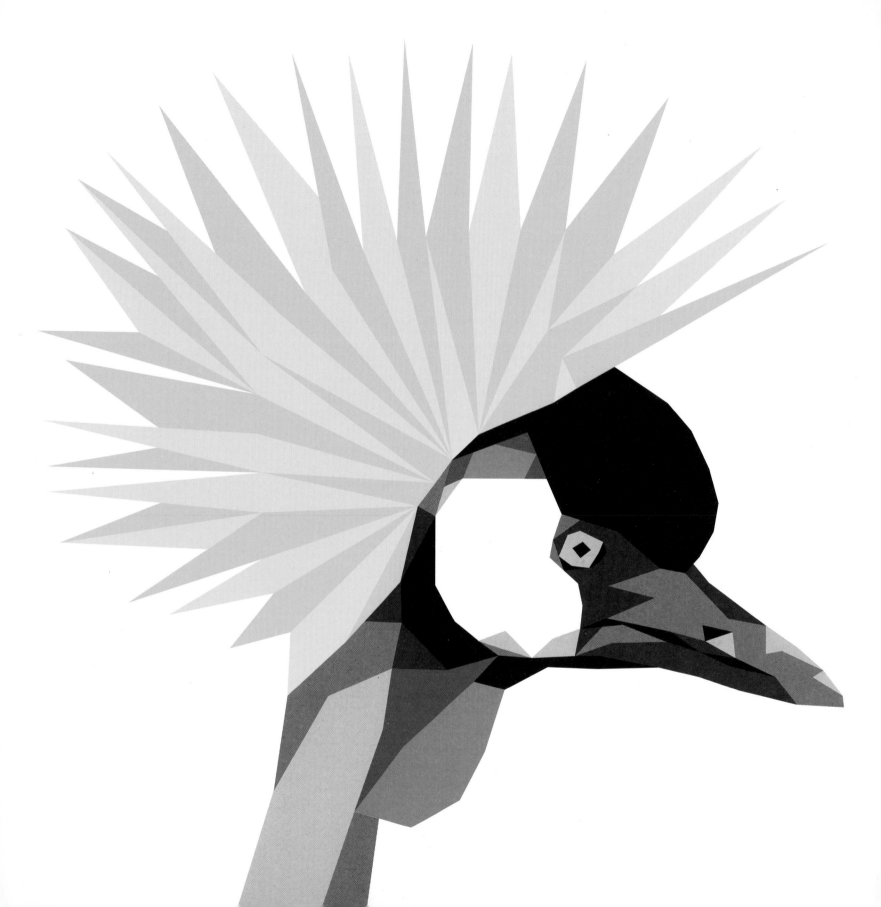

LET'S GET WILD!

Welcome to the wonderful world of *Trianimals*. In this book you will find a whole menagerie of wild animals that have been illustrated using hundreds of triangles of varying sizes. Whether it's a red panda, mountain goat, chameleon, meerkat, buffalo, or penguin, it's time to choose your favorite animal and get coloring.

The colors used in the palettes are as close to the real thing as possible, meaning that these exciting creatures come to life on every page. Each animal in the book has very different facial features, attitudes, patterns, color combinations, and characteristics—carefully color in the images and watch as the animals start to reveal themselves, leaping out of the pages in glorious technicolor.

Coloring is the perfect pastime, aiding relaxation and allowing you to focus all your energy on a calm, quiet activity. So lose yourself in the pages of this book and discover talents you never knew you had. You can also join us online! Share your colored-in animal on social media using the hashtag #Trianimals.

FROM THE AUTHORS

When thinking about creating this book, we found inspiration in many areas: the natural world, photographs online, and also computer graphics. We wanted to experiment, test our capabilities, and this book is the result. Why triangles? It's the shape that offers the most variety, they work very well together, and enable us to create complex images of each animal's head by using different sizes and combinations.

We have always loved wild animals so were naturally drawn to using them as our subject matter. They are all so different, with unique characteristics, colors, and personalities. We hope you enjoy coloring them as much as we enjoyed creating them.

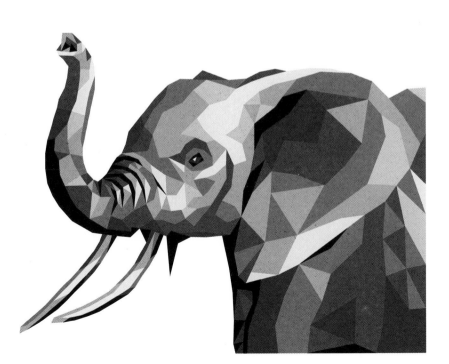

MATERIALS

Invest in a pack of colored pencils or felt-tip pens, and try to replicate the lightness and darkness of each shade. It's the light and dark triangles sitting side by side that give the images their depth and amazing 3-D look.

If you don't have colored pencils or felt-tip pens, you could try watercolors or paint, and mix your own colors to create the right shade. But stay away from pastels as these are quite thick and it will be difficult to fill in the smaller triangles. Avoid charcoal too as this is likely to smudge, ruining all your hard work.

TECHNIQUES

Stay inside the lines and keep your pencils sharp so you have maximum control in the smaller areas. Sharpen your pencils frequently to achieve crisp, clean images.

If the color of your pencil doesn't quite match our color palette, try blending, cross-hatching, and adding more layers until you get the color you want. Take your time—a masterpiece was never created in a day!

If you are struggling to create a particular shade, try substituting that color for one you have available, or you could create your own color palette, just remember to keep dark shades dark and light shades light.

To achieve a darker shade, try layering the color until you get the right shade. Pressing harder with your colored pencil should also achieve this result.

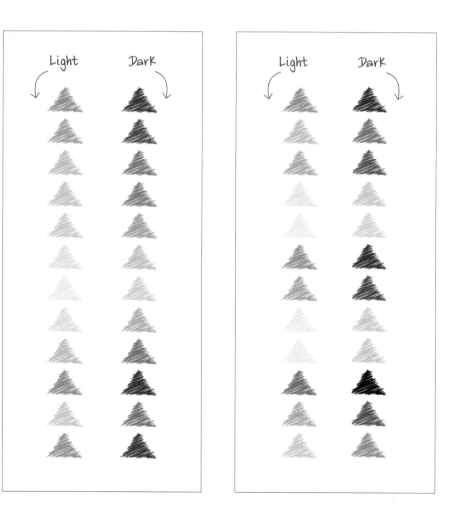

USING THE COLOR PALETTE

Two color palettes have been created alongside the illustrations in this book. The natural palette is based on the animal's natural coloring and the vivid palette can be used to create a more vibrant and graphic look.

NO NUMBER?
On the main illustration, if a triangle doesn't have a number that area is white, so there is no need to color it in.

USING THE NATURAL PALETTE
The key to getting your animals to look like the original image is to follow the natural palette as closely as possible.

USING THE VIVID PALETTE
If you're looking for something a bit brighter, or just a bit different, try our vivid color palettes.

FREESTYLING
Avid colorers will spot that there are no color palettes on the patterned pages for the poison dart frog, koala, or red squirrel. There are also "color me in" versions of the openers for each section. These animals have been left unnumbered so you can let your imagination run wild.

This is your chance to experiment with different colors and techniques. Why not create your own color palette around your favorite color, or create a wacky pattern using a pop art style?

For the best results, think about your shading. Imagine where the sun would catch the animal in real life and try to keep those areas lighter than areas in the shade. The diagrams on page 12 show how the same color can be used in different ways to achieve this.

Look out for the animal's natural color palette at the top of each design.

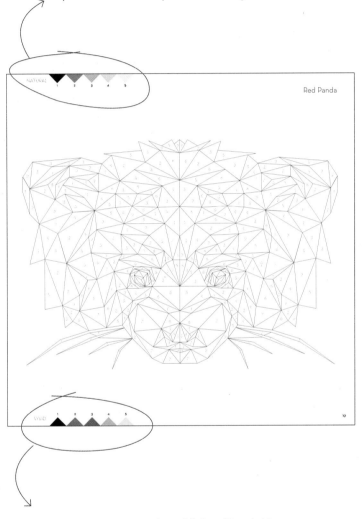

Red Panda

Are you ready to experiment? Try the vivid color palette at the bottom of the page.

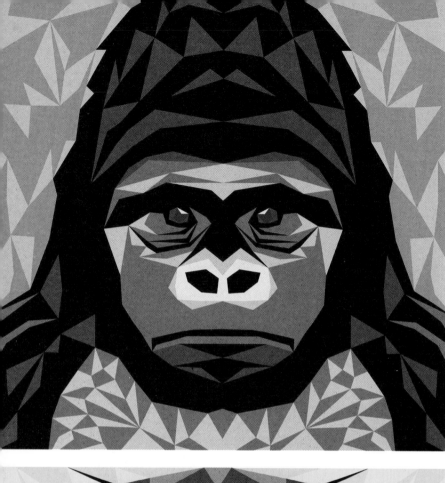
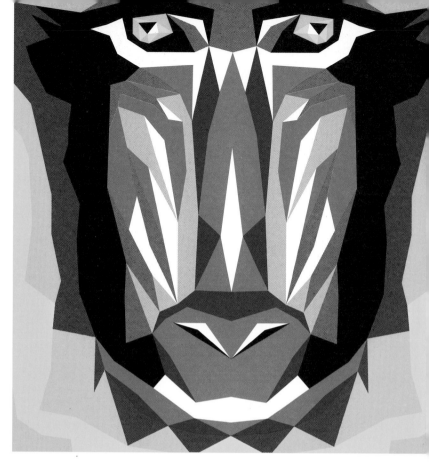
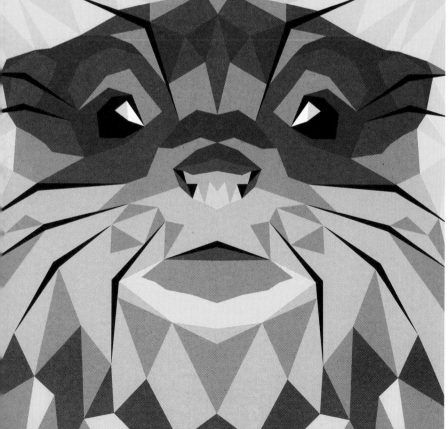
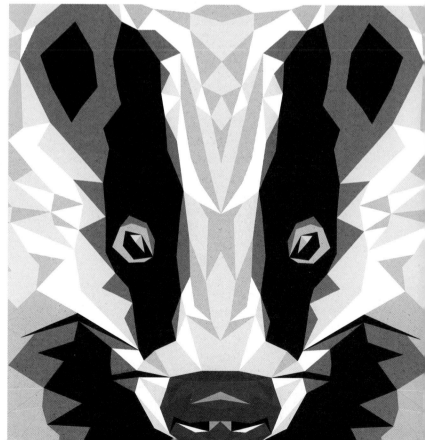

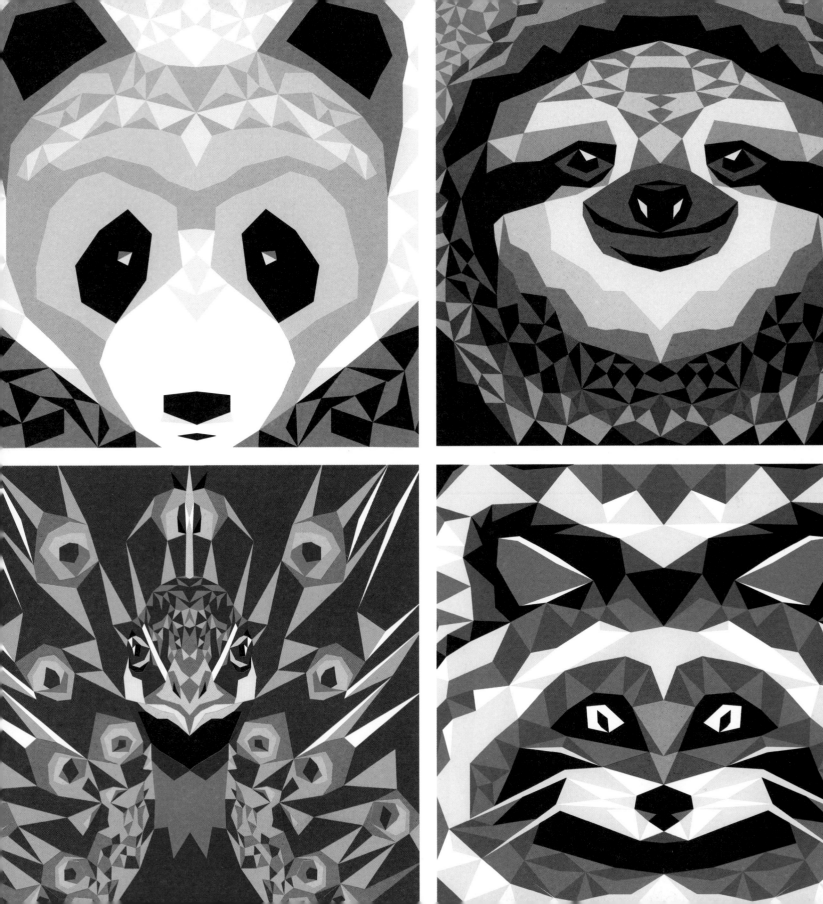

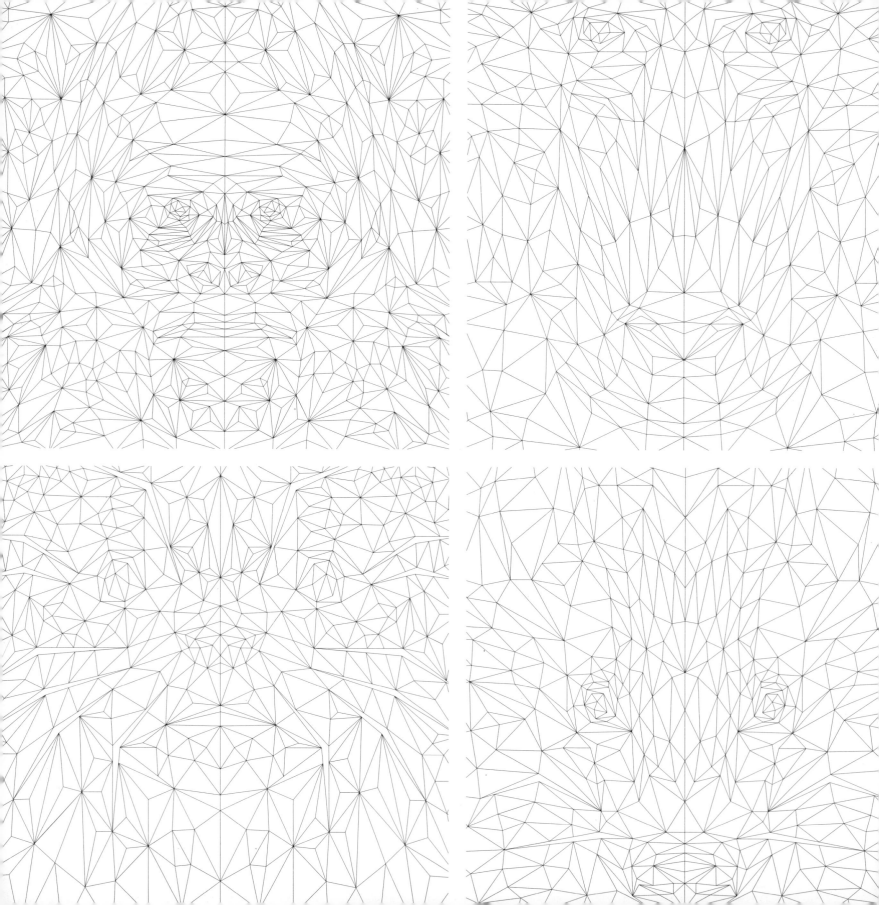

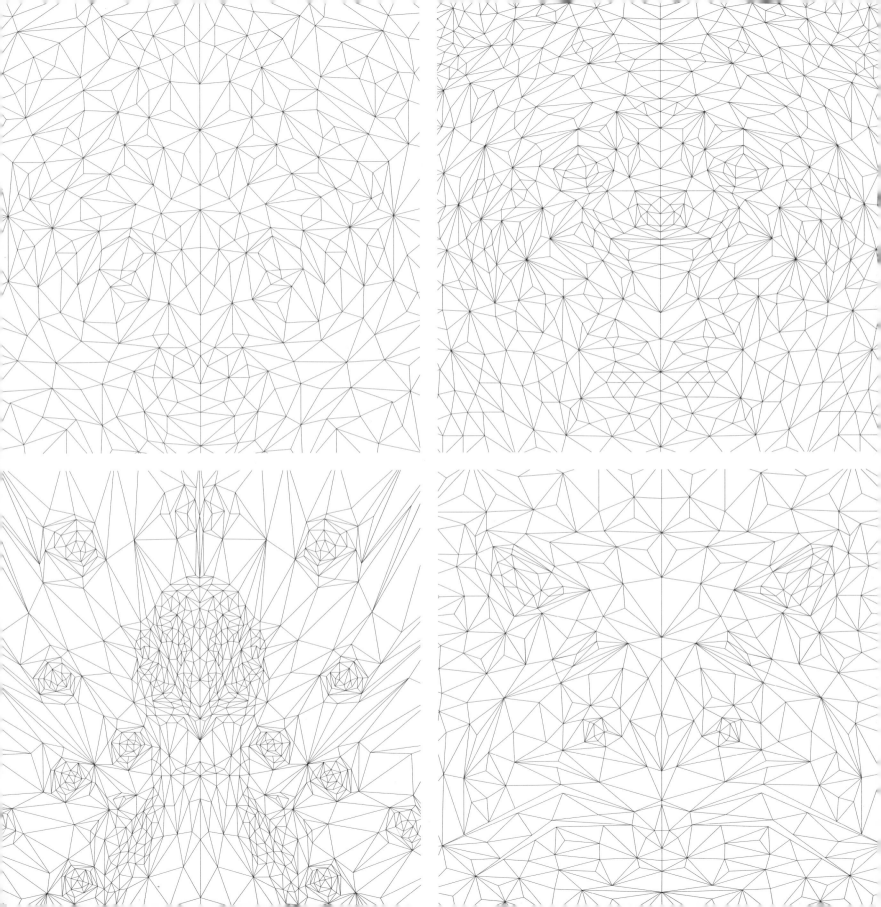

Raccoon

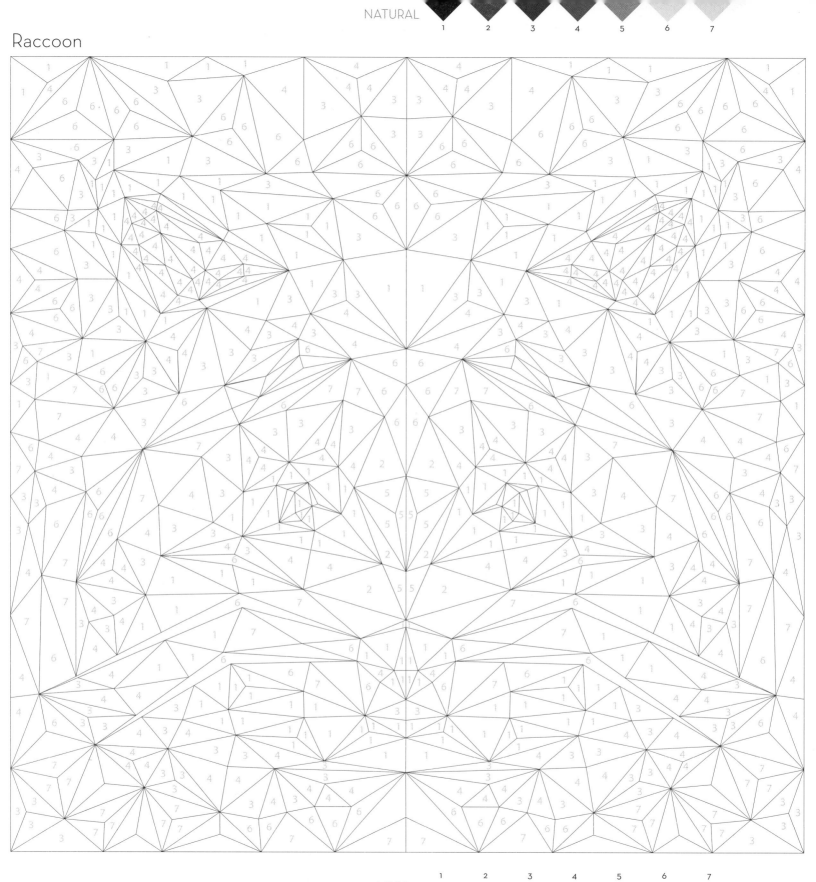

Yak

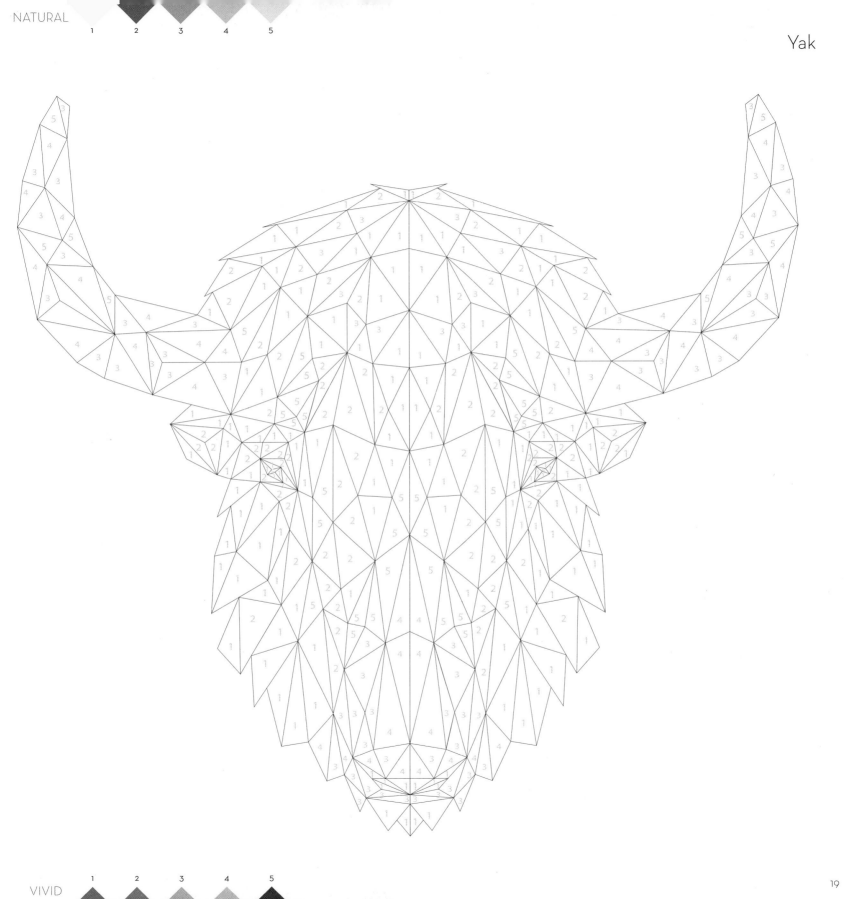

Iguana

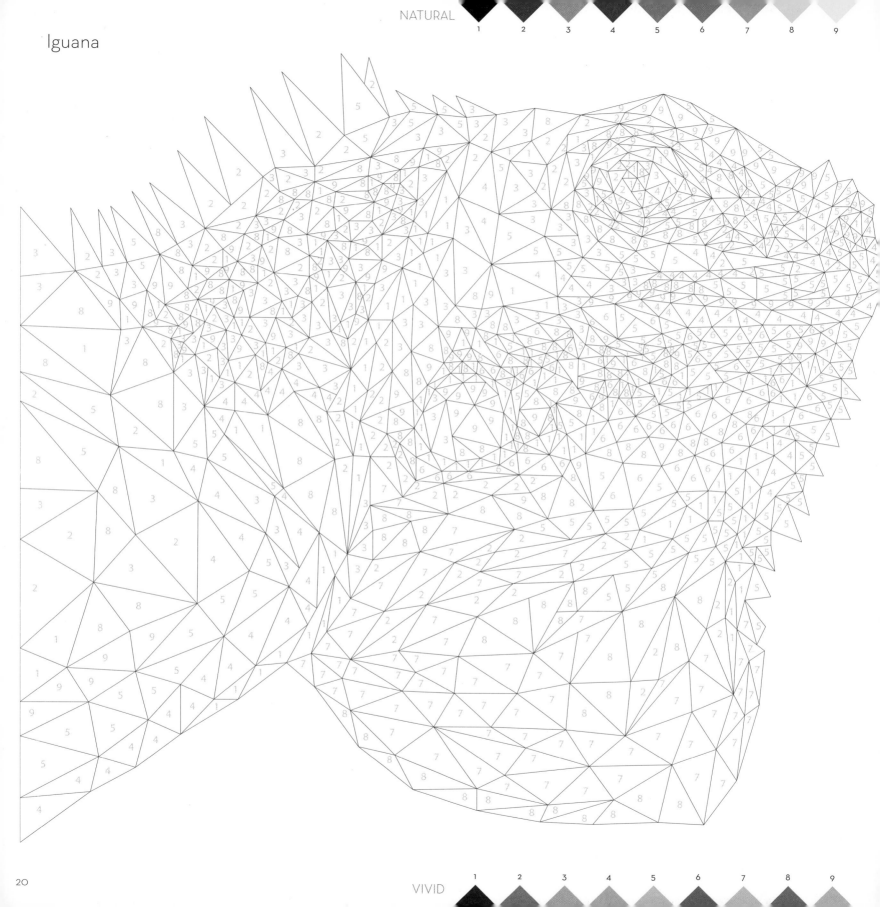

Red Panda

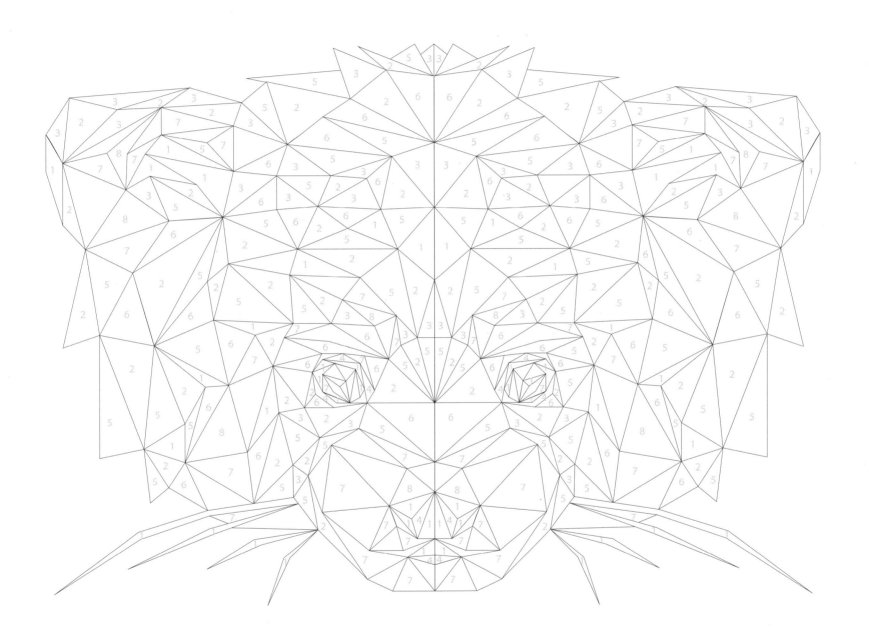

Lemur

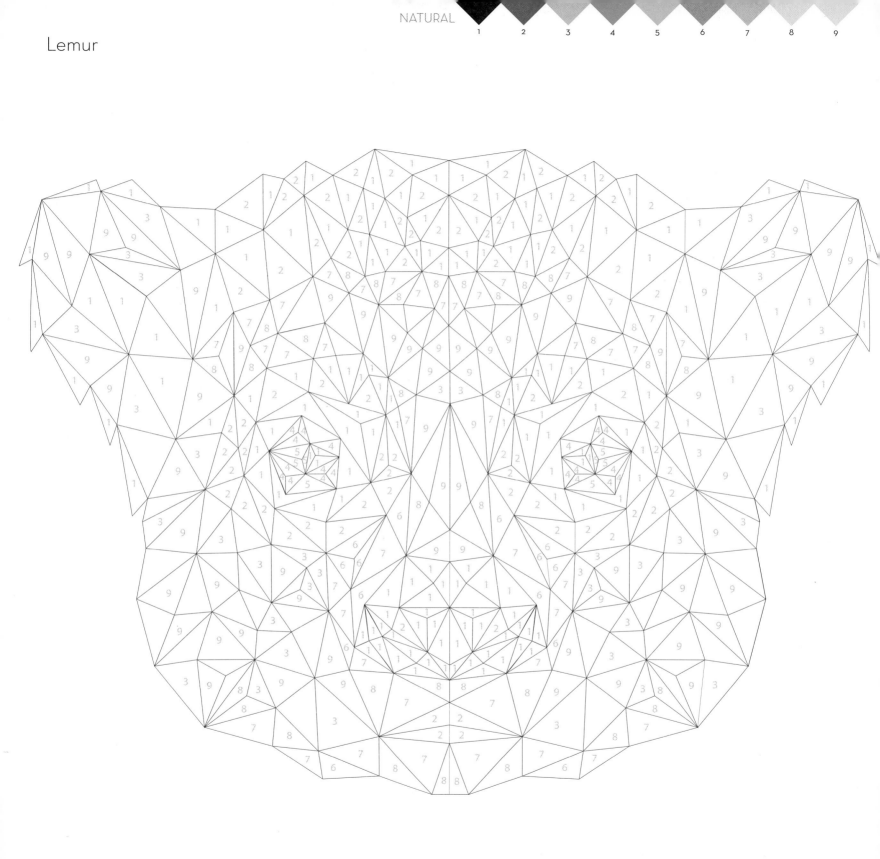

Peacock

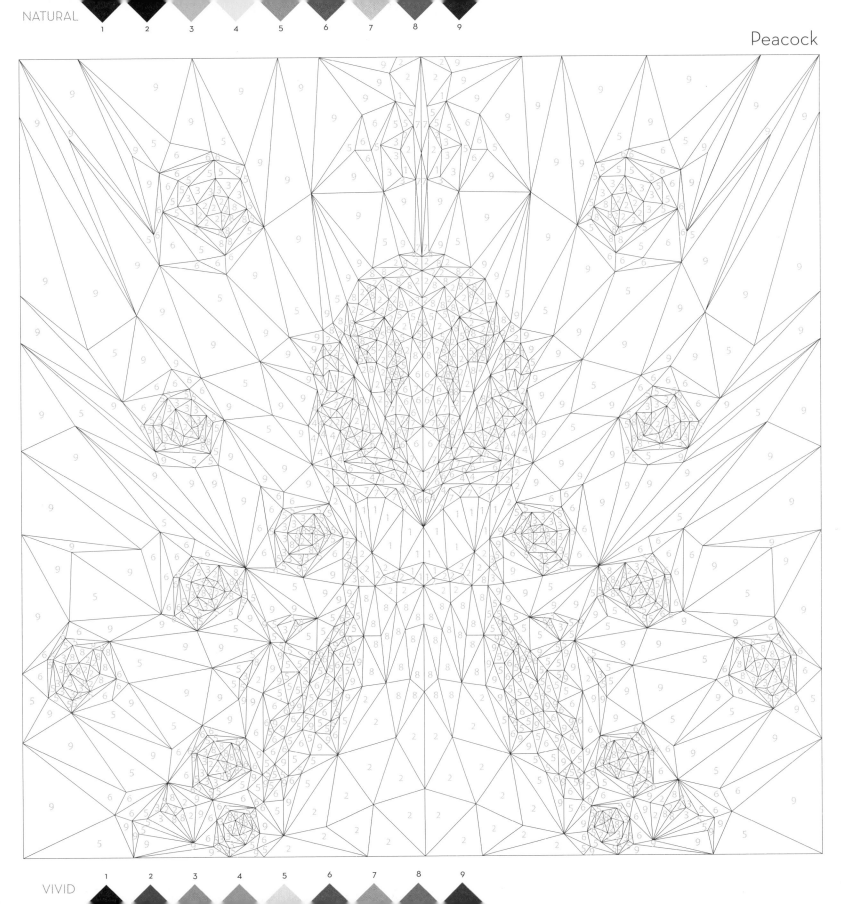

Crested Crane

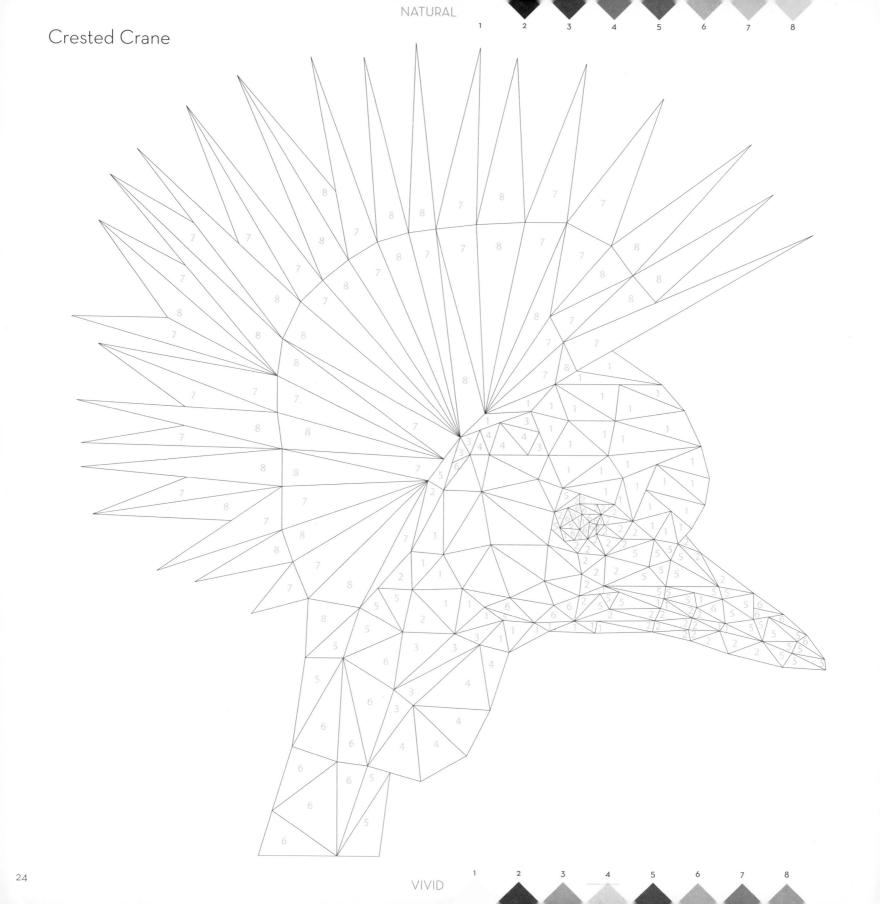

Slow Loris

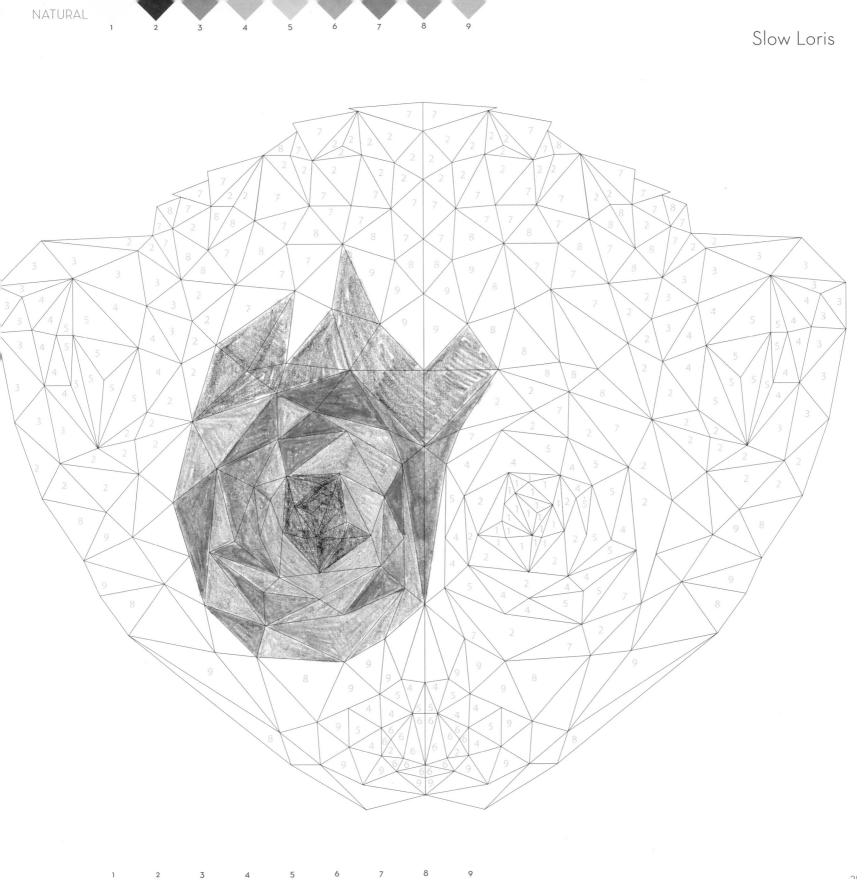

Poison Dart Frog

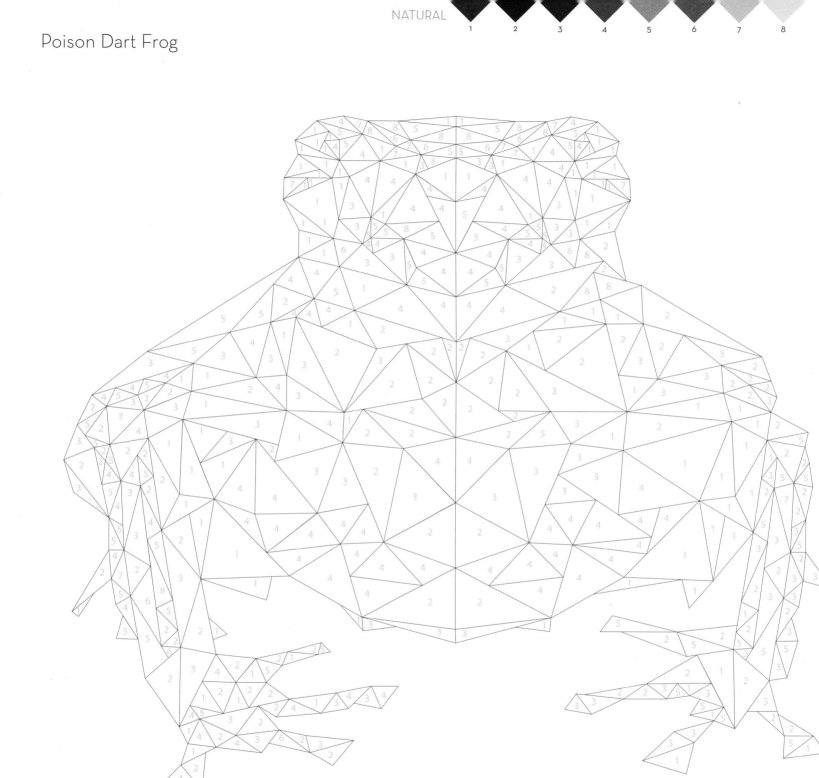

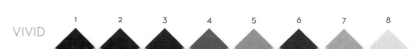

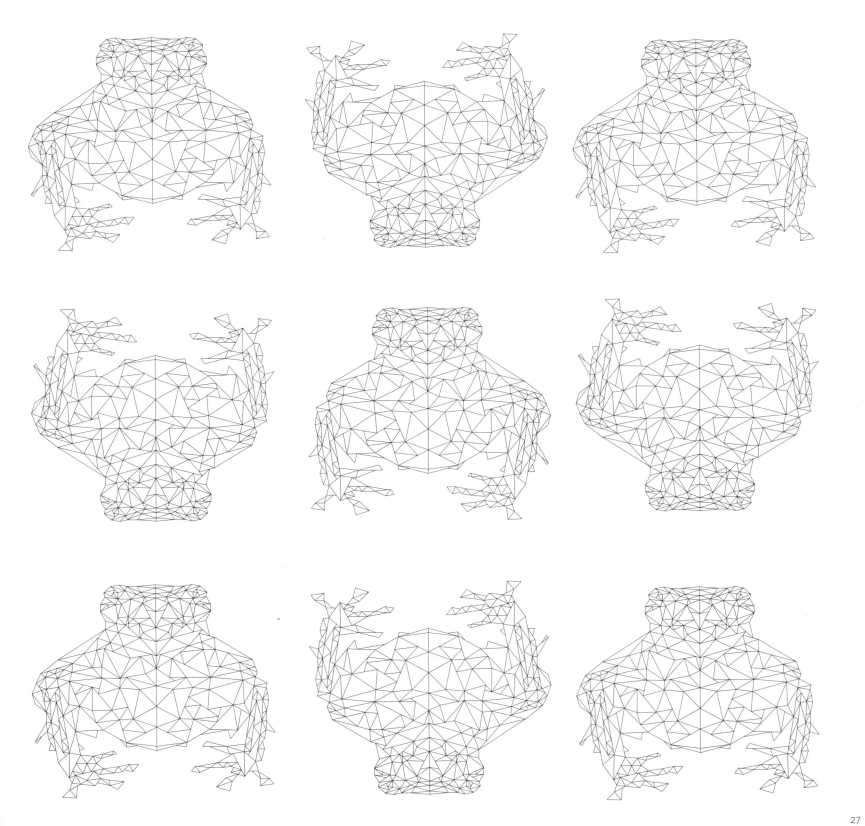

Stag

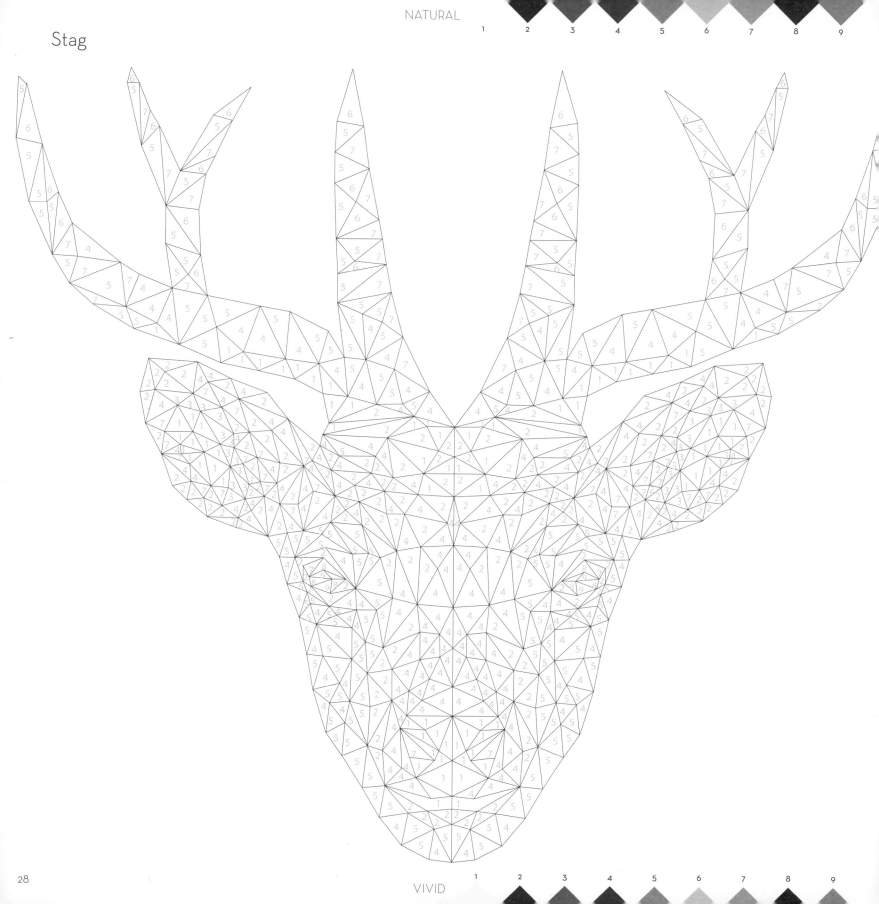

Meerkat

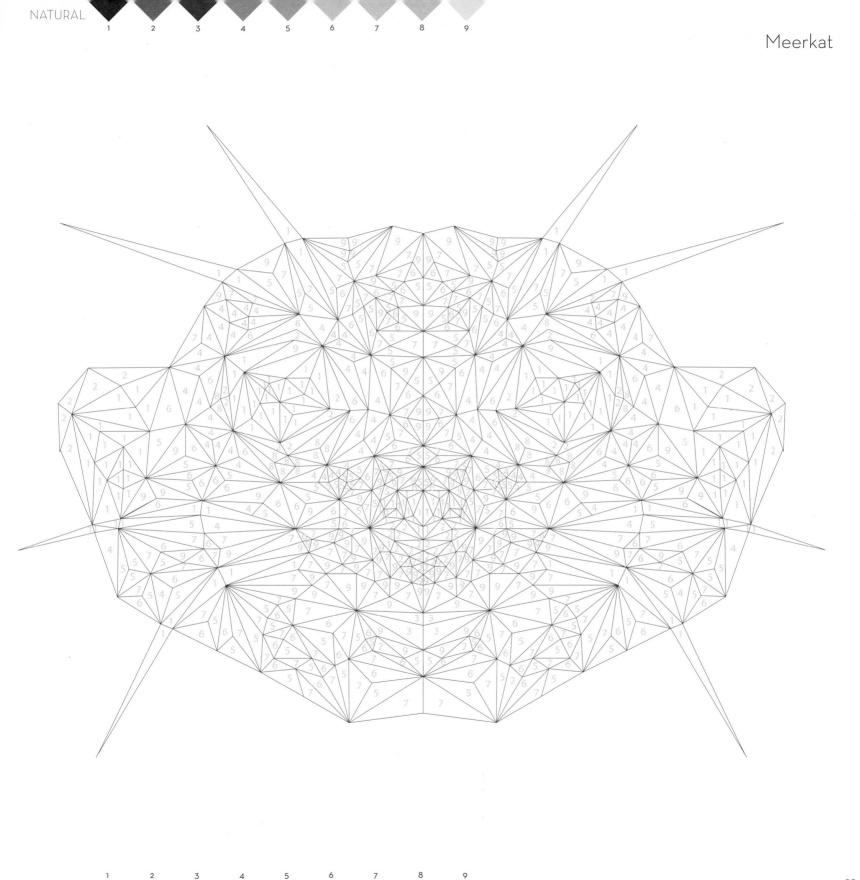

Mountain Goat

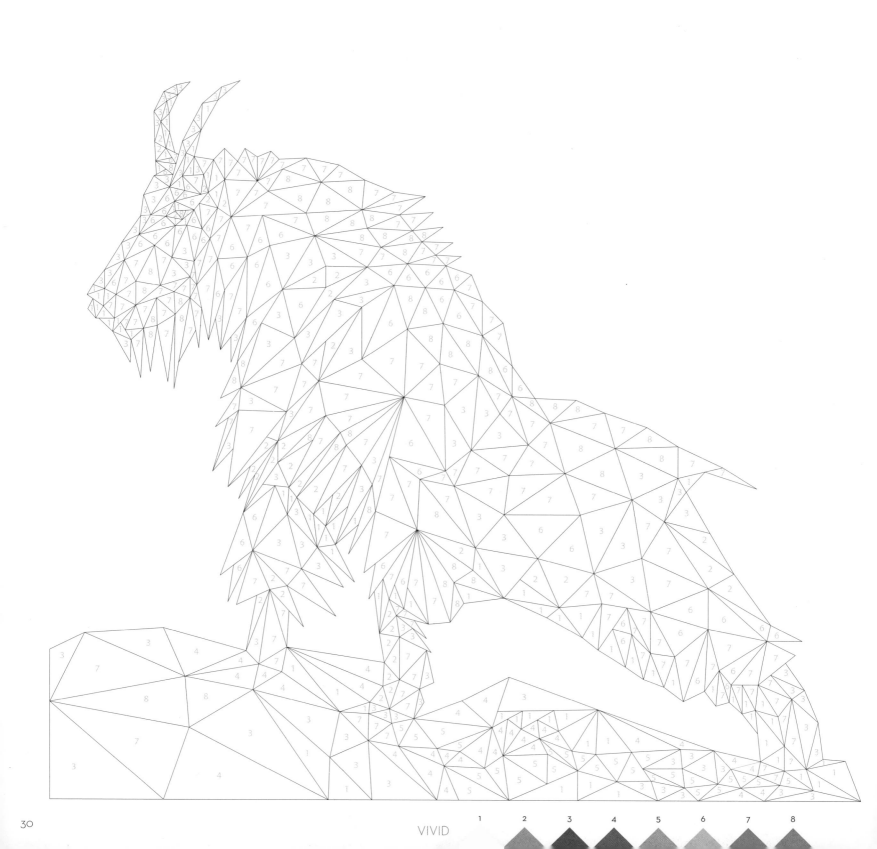

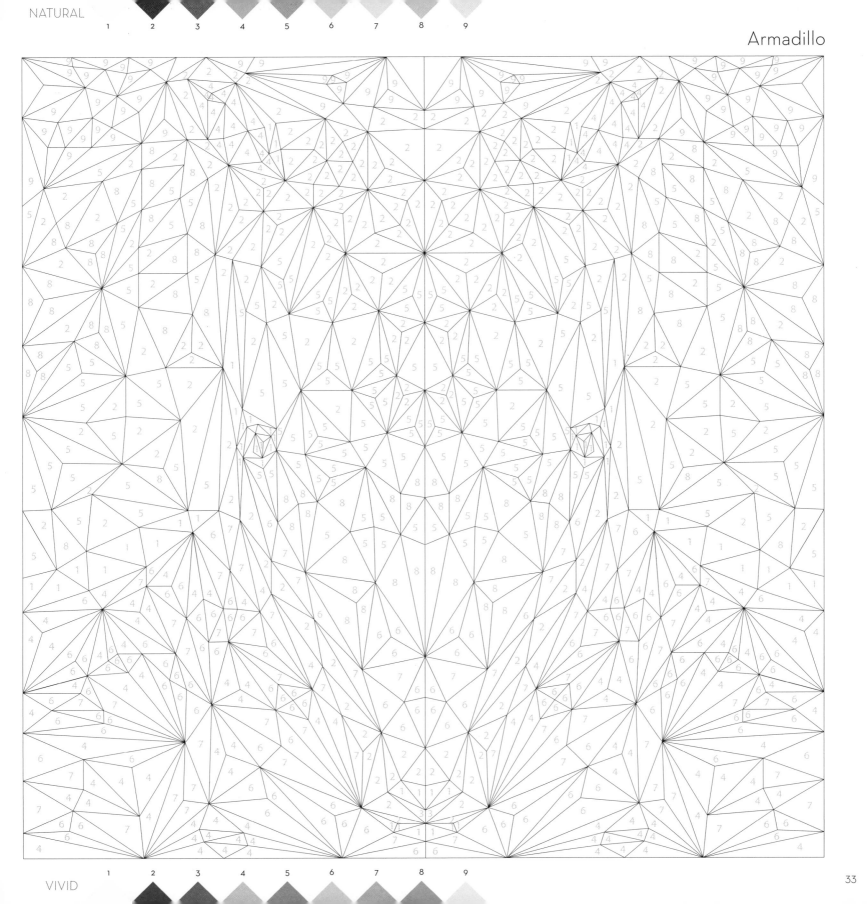

Armadillo

Giraffe

NATURAL

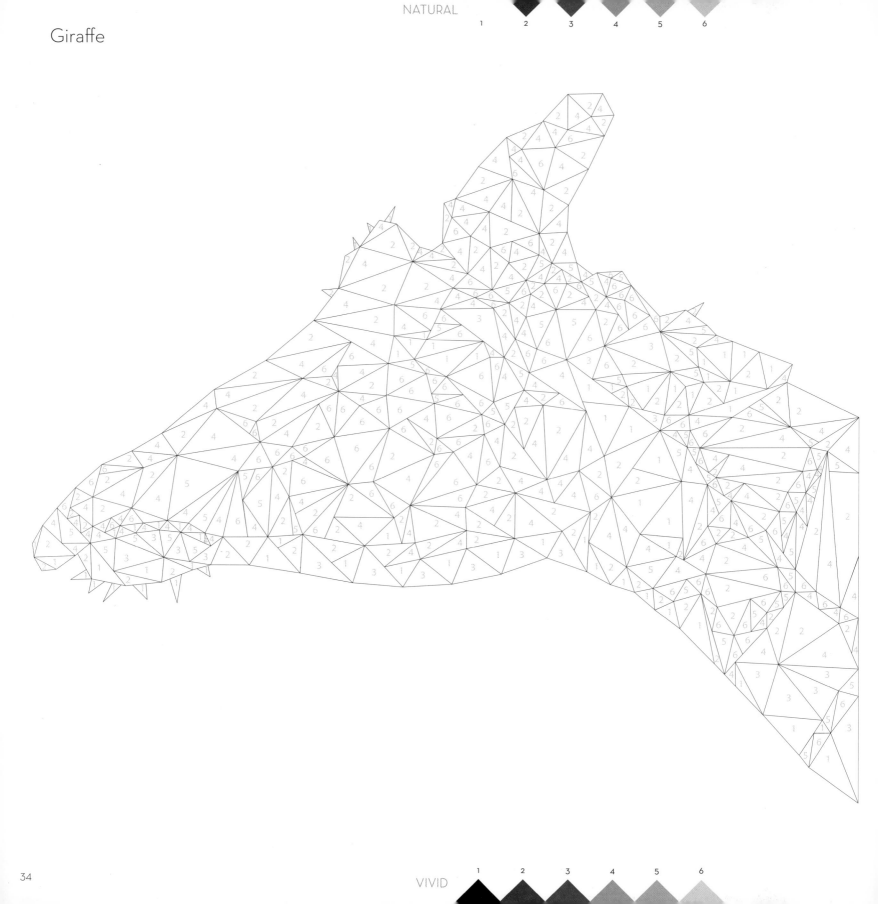

VIVID

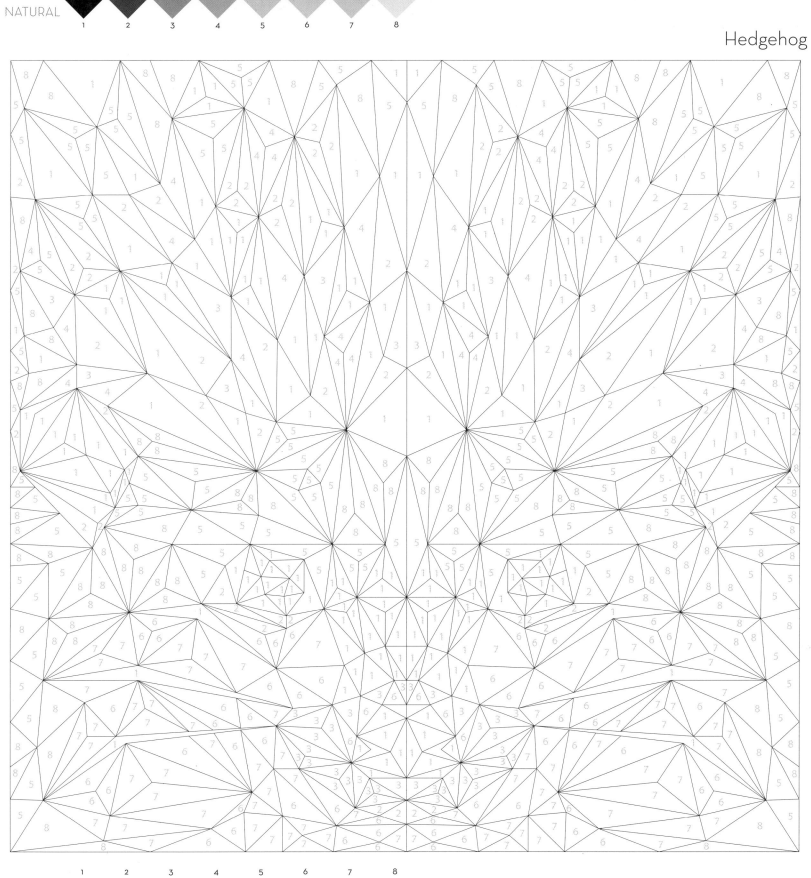

Anteater

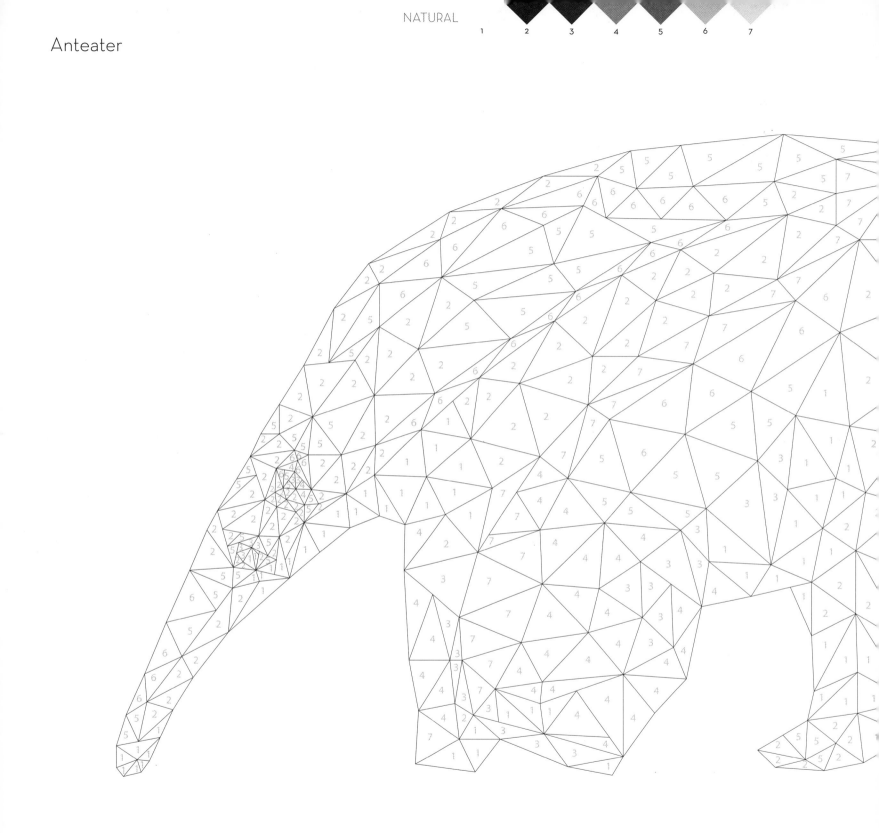

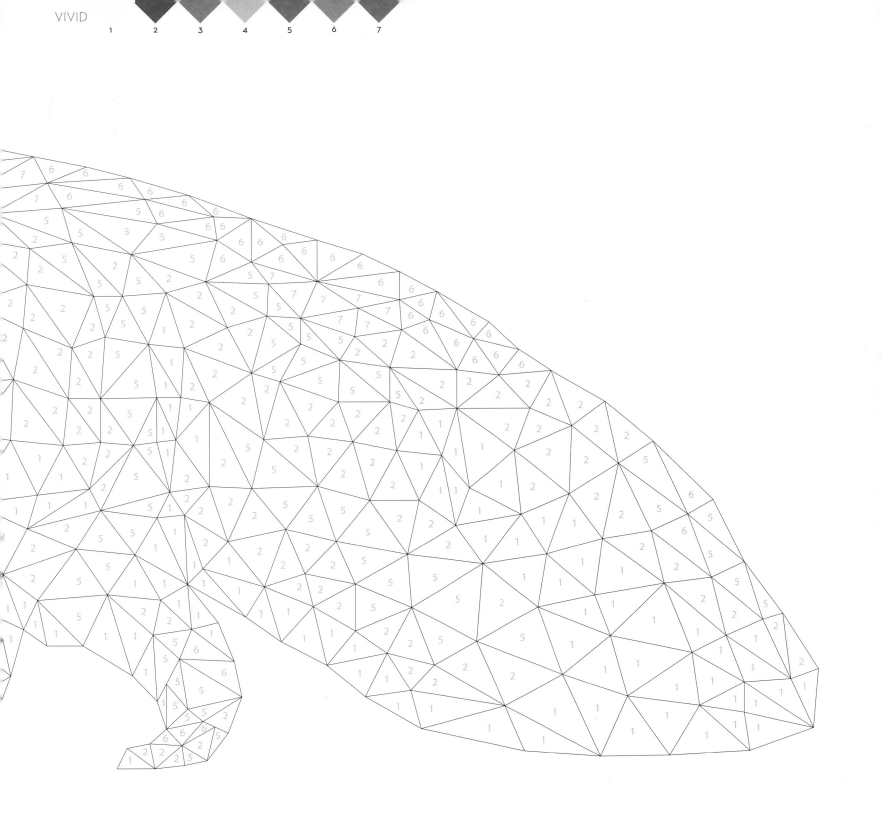

Aye-aye

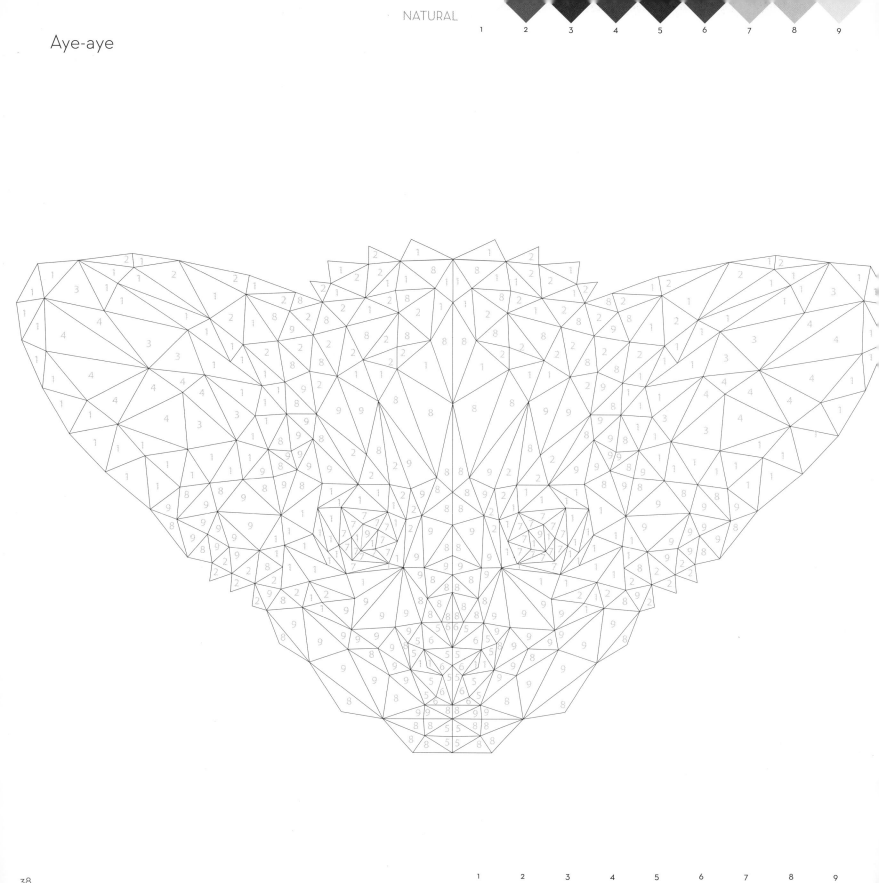

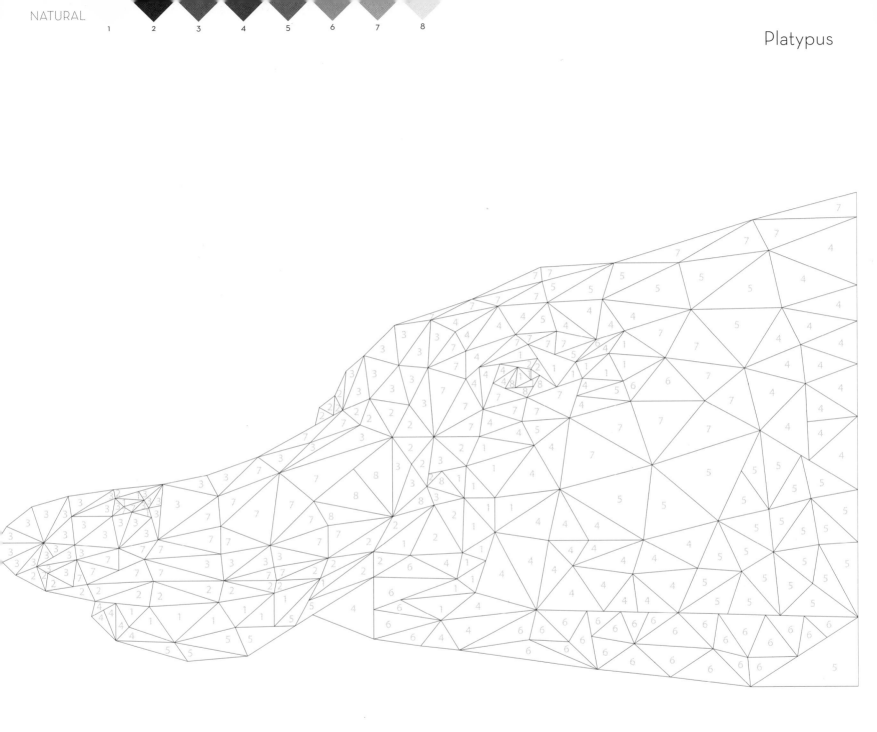

Common Seal

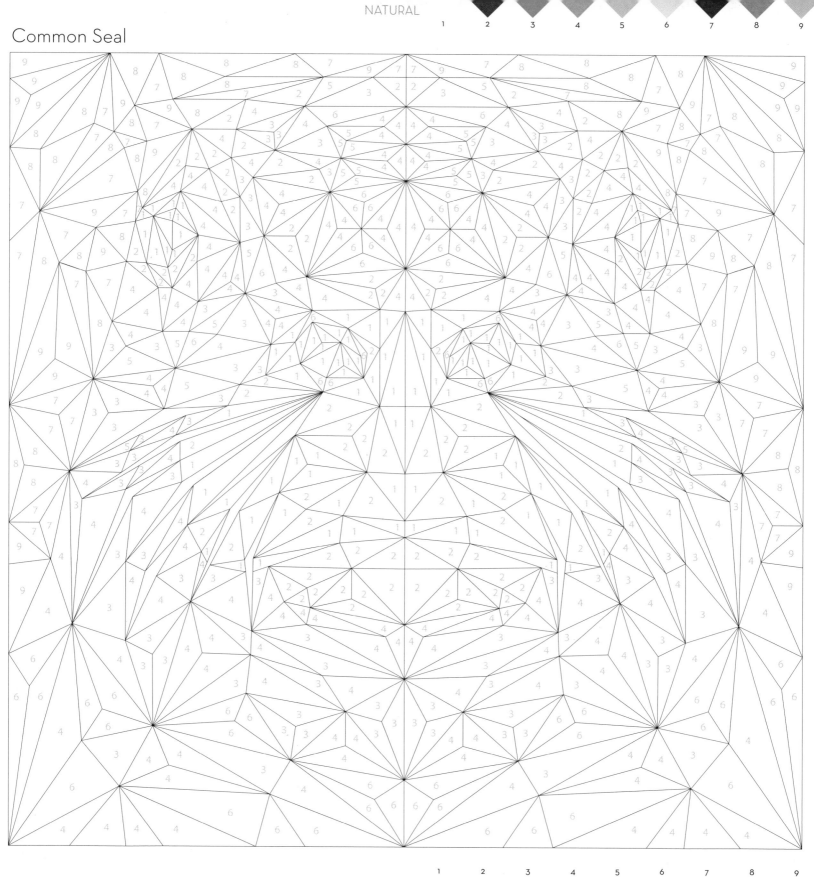

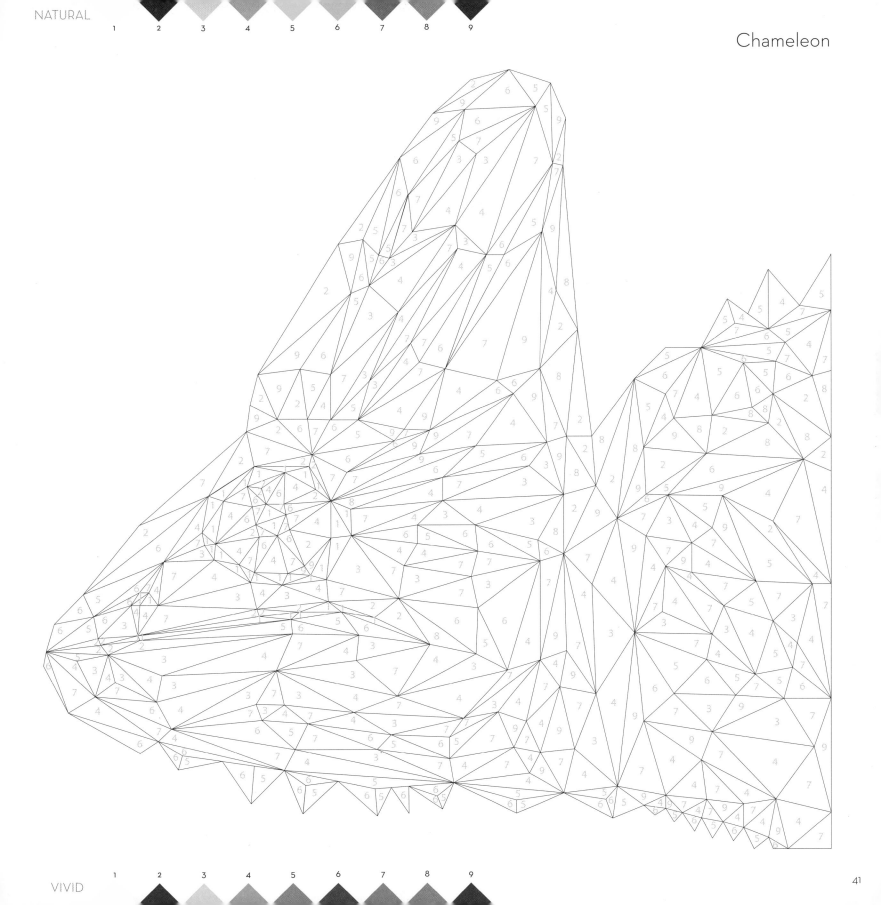

Chameleon

Sloth

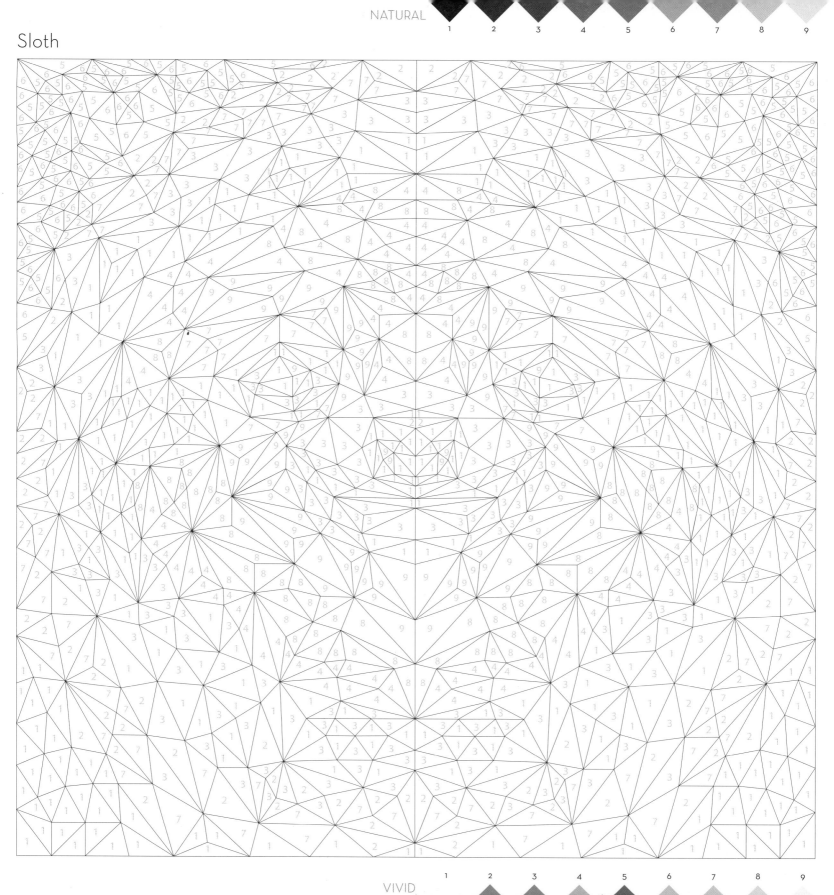

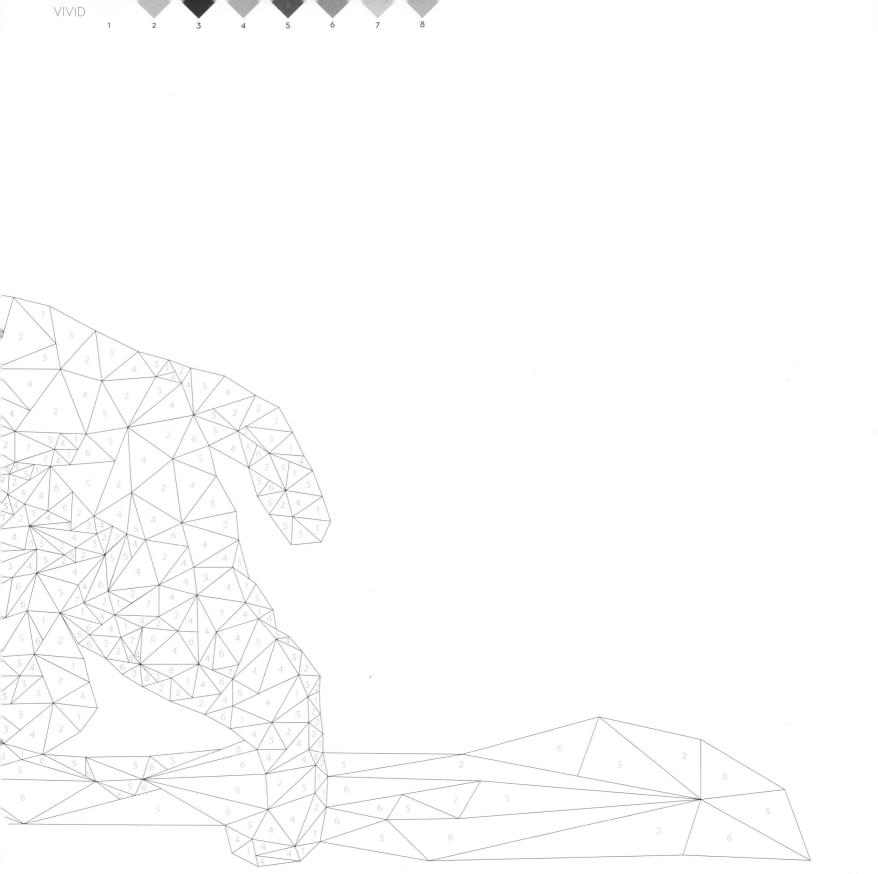

Otter

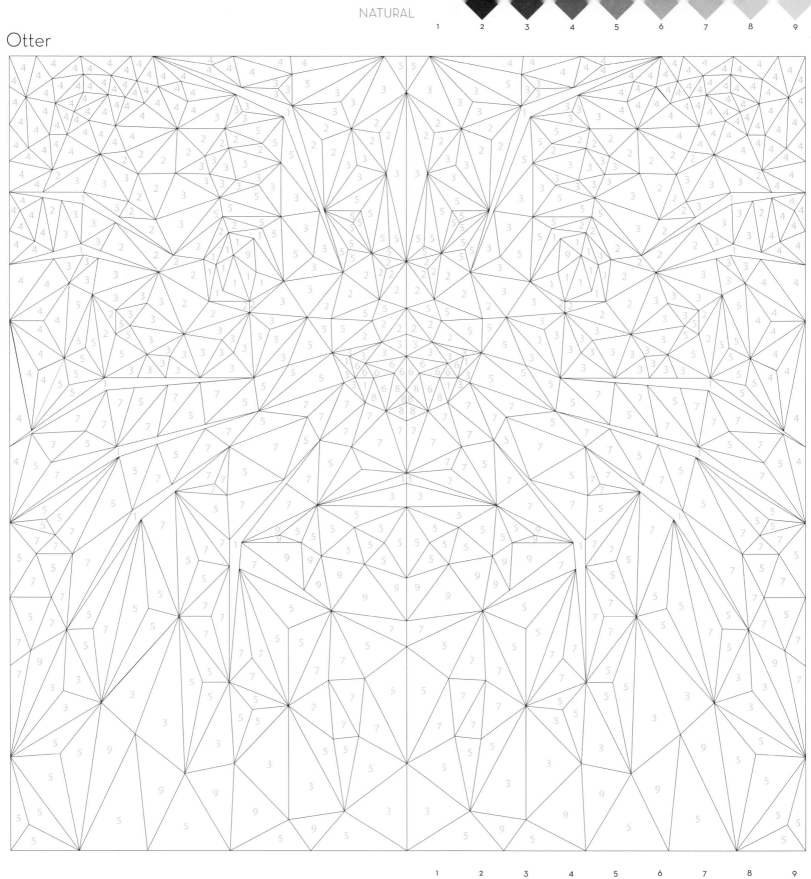

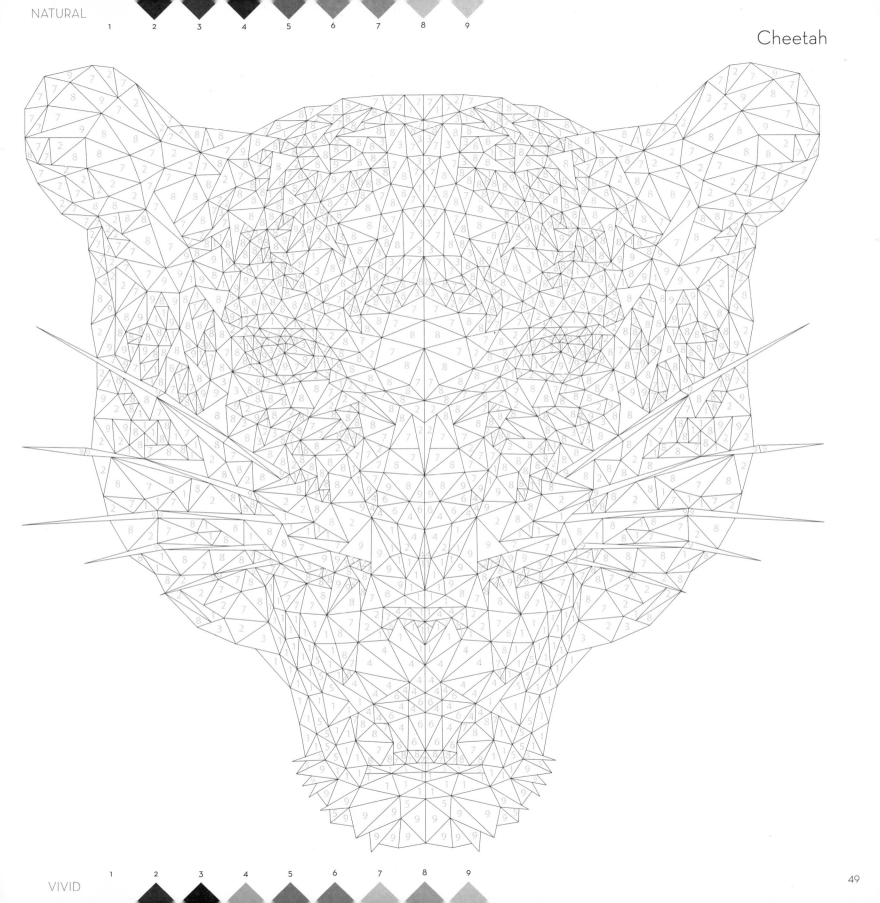

Cheetah

Tortoise

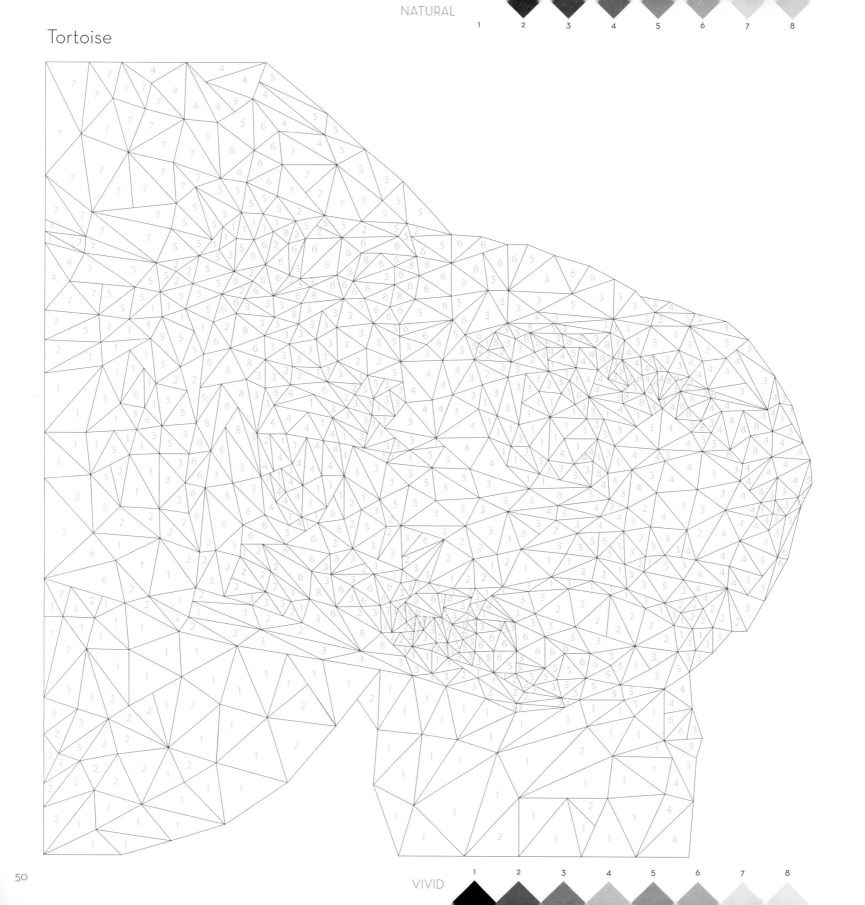

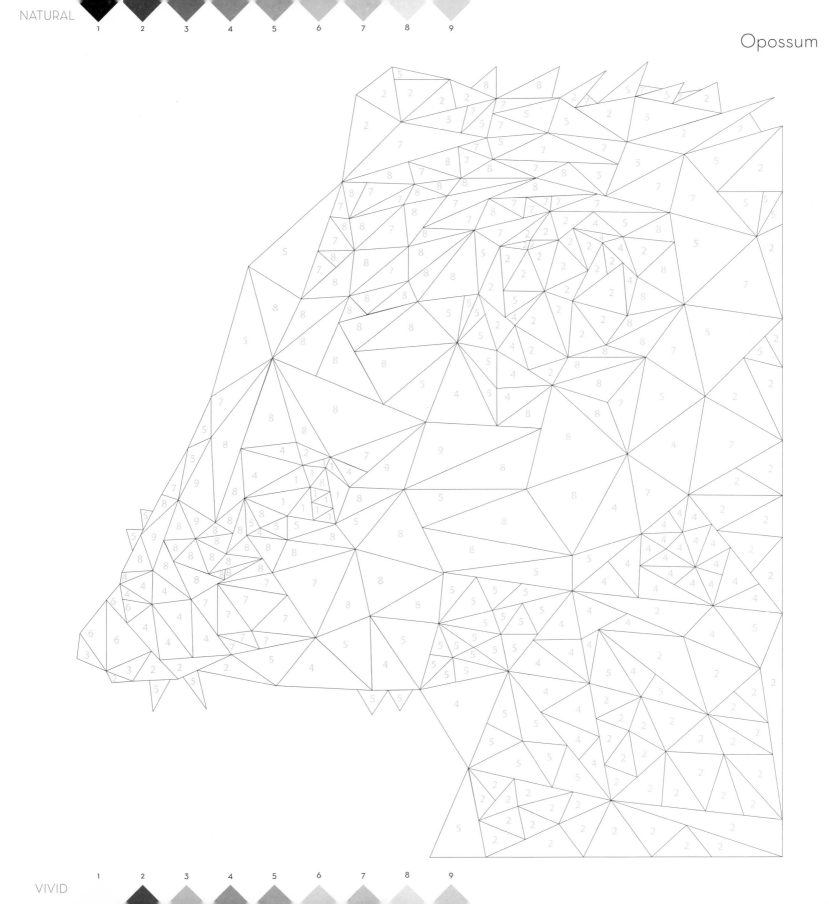

Brown Bear

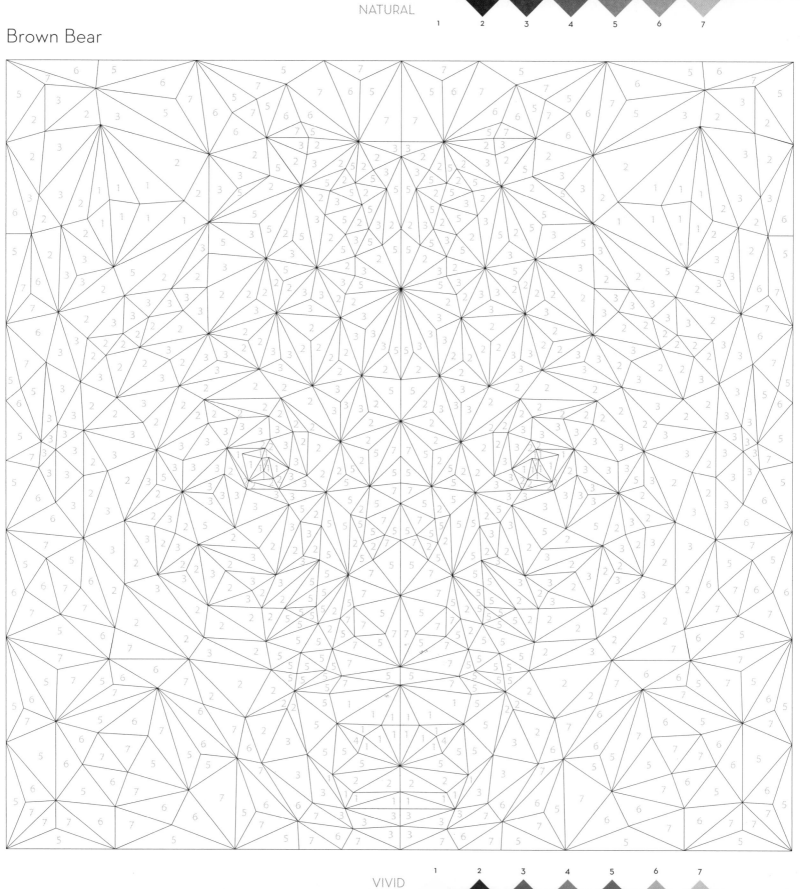

Mandrill

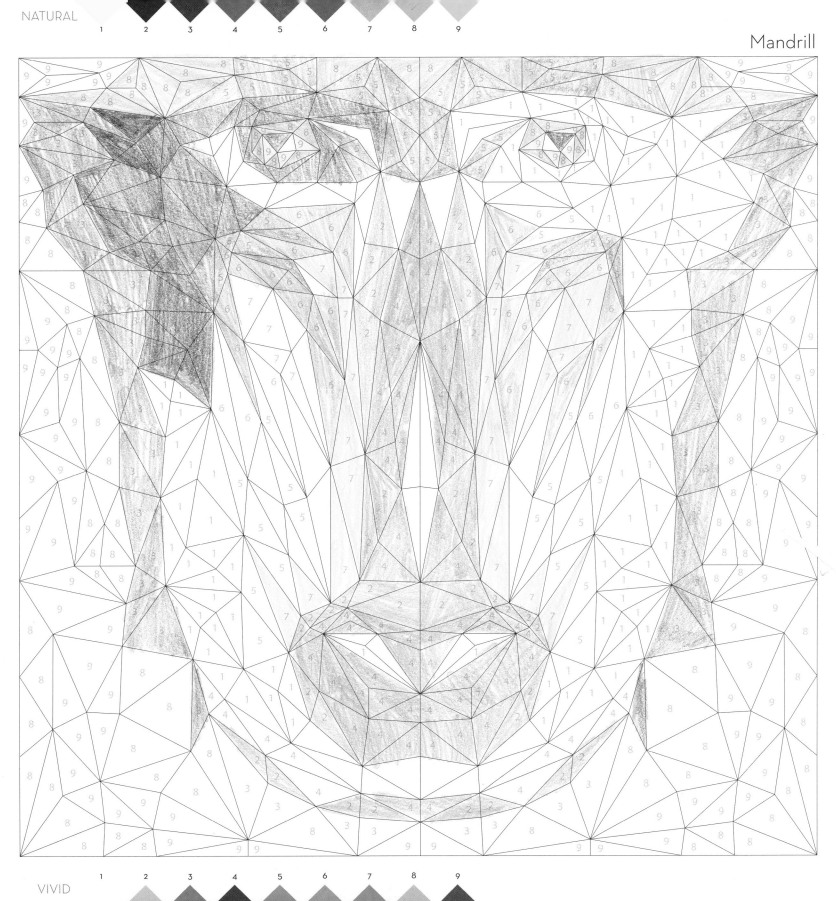

Koala

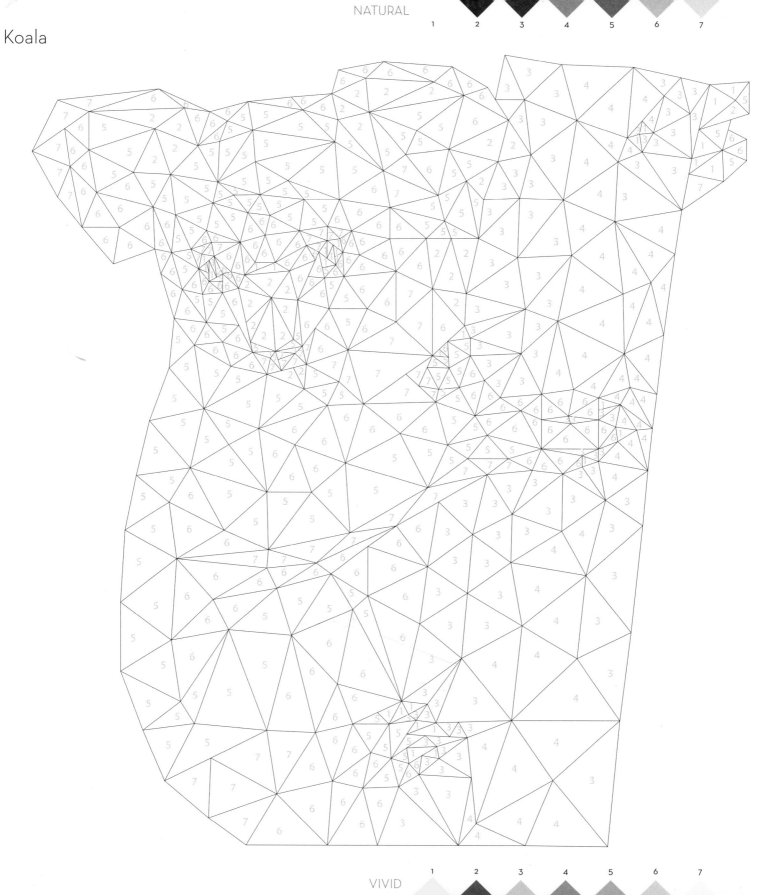

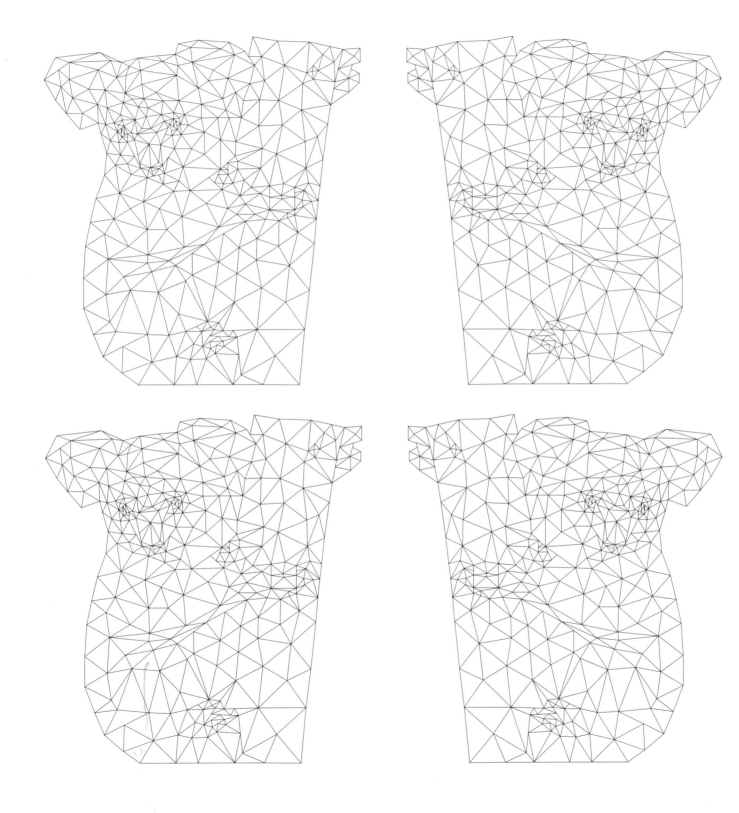

Alligator

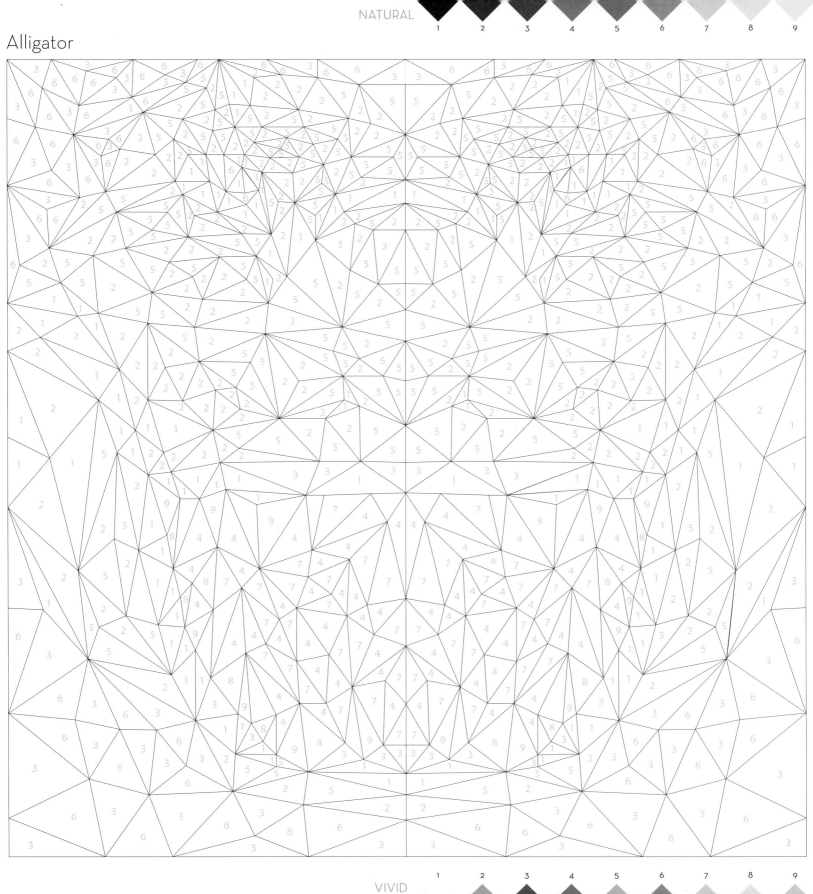

Fox

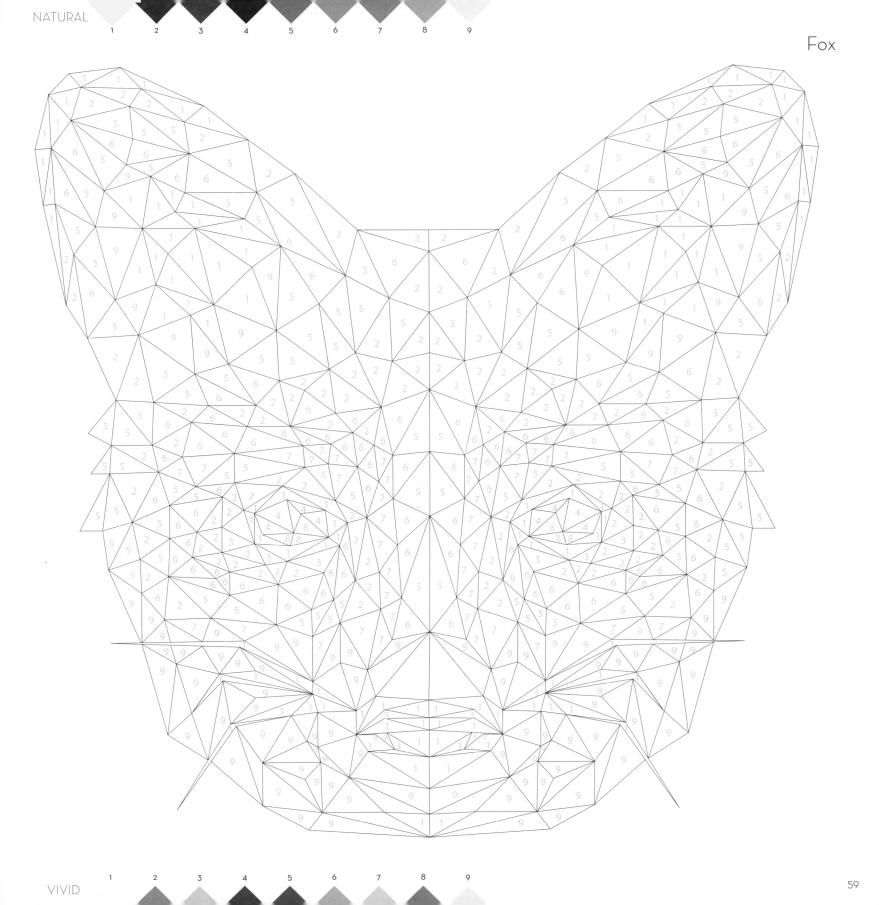

Llama

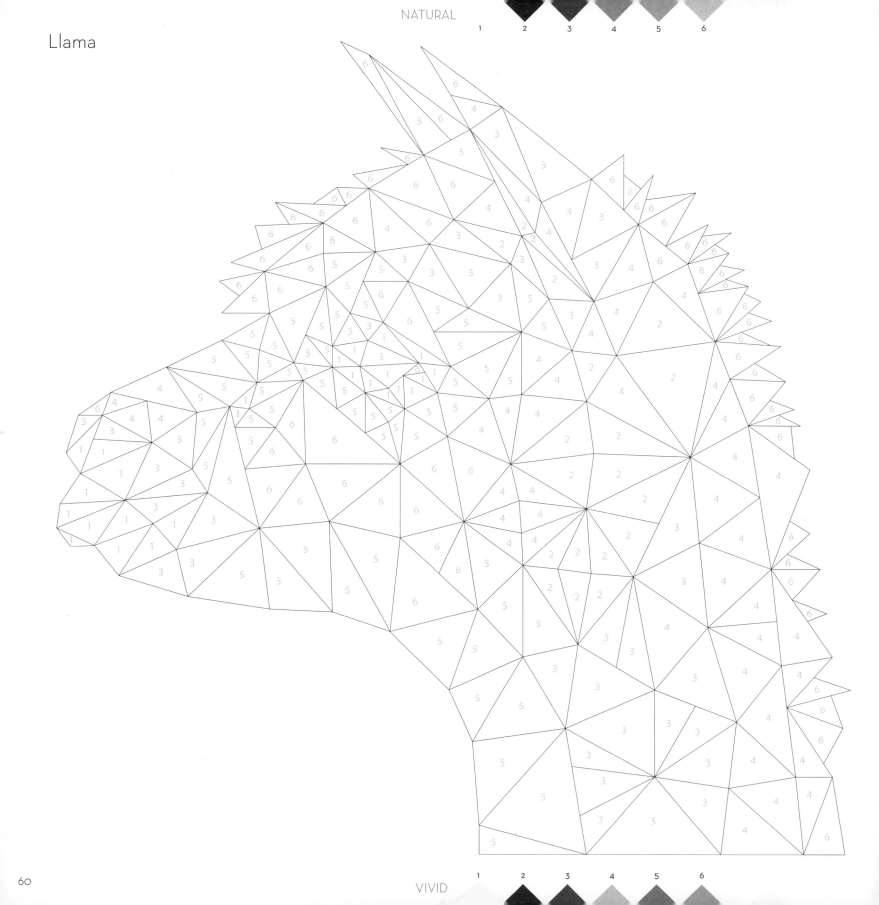

Camel

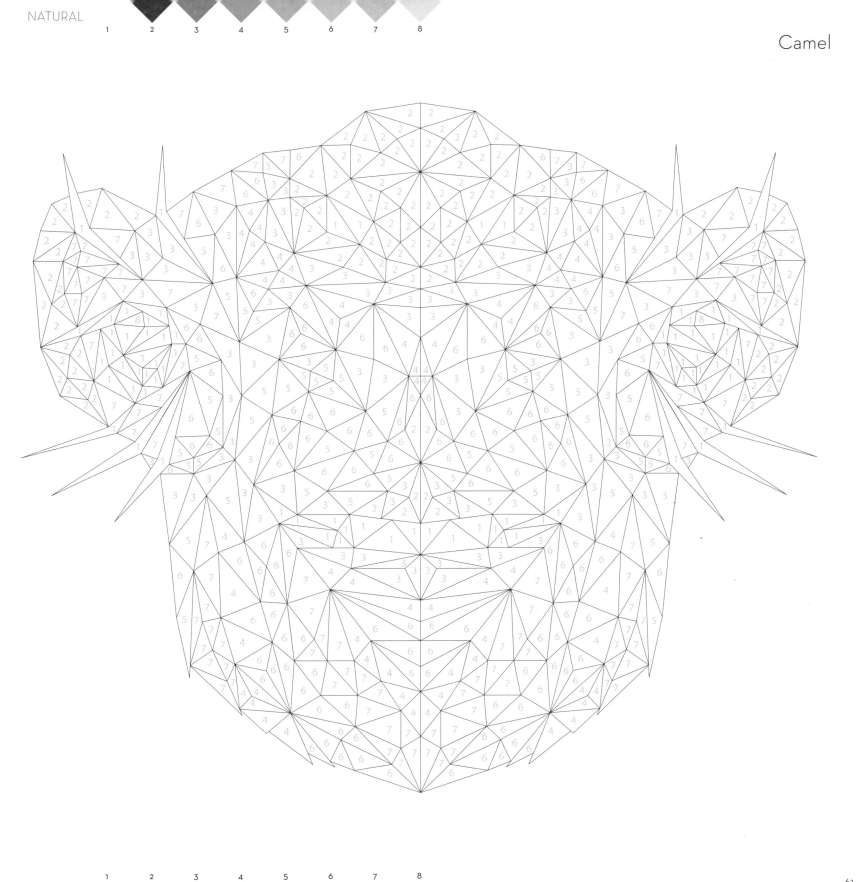

Badger

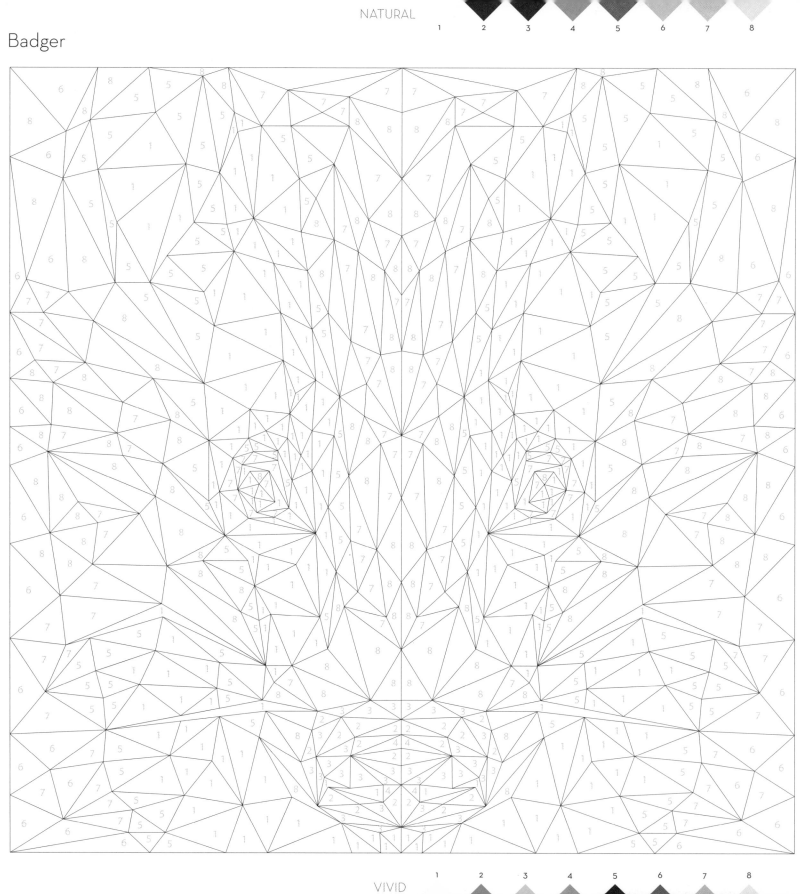

Beaver

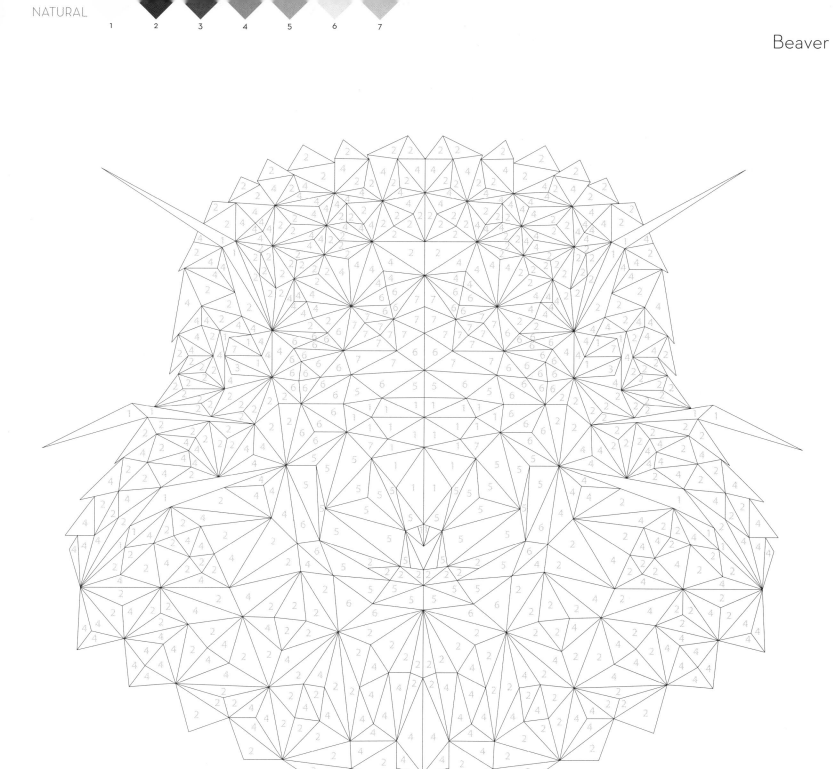

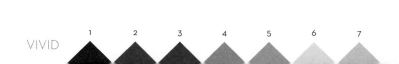

Elephant

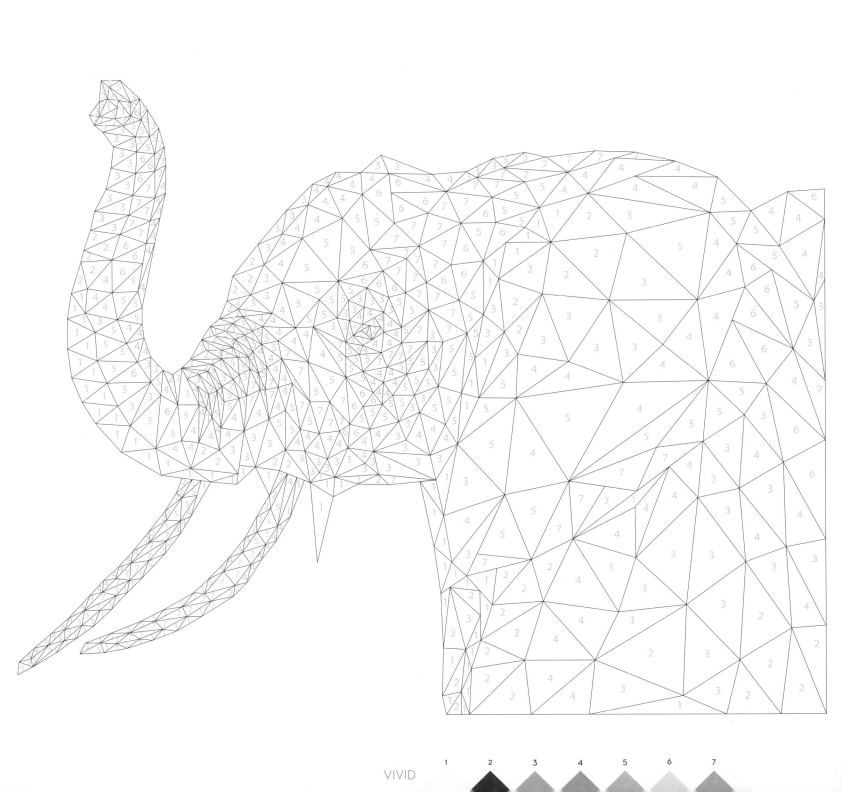

Kangaroo

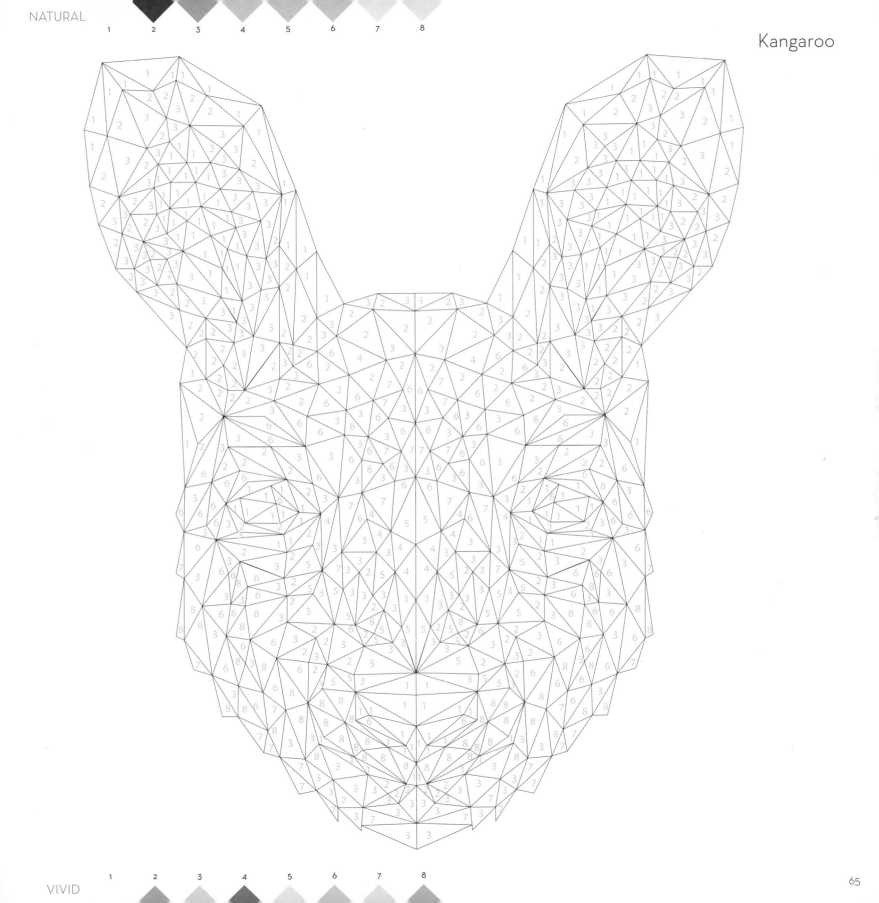

Red Squirrel

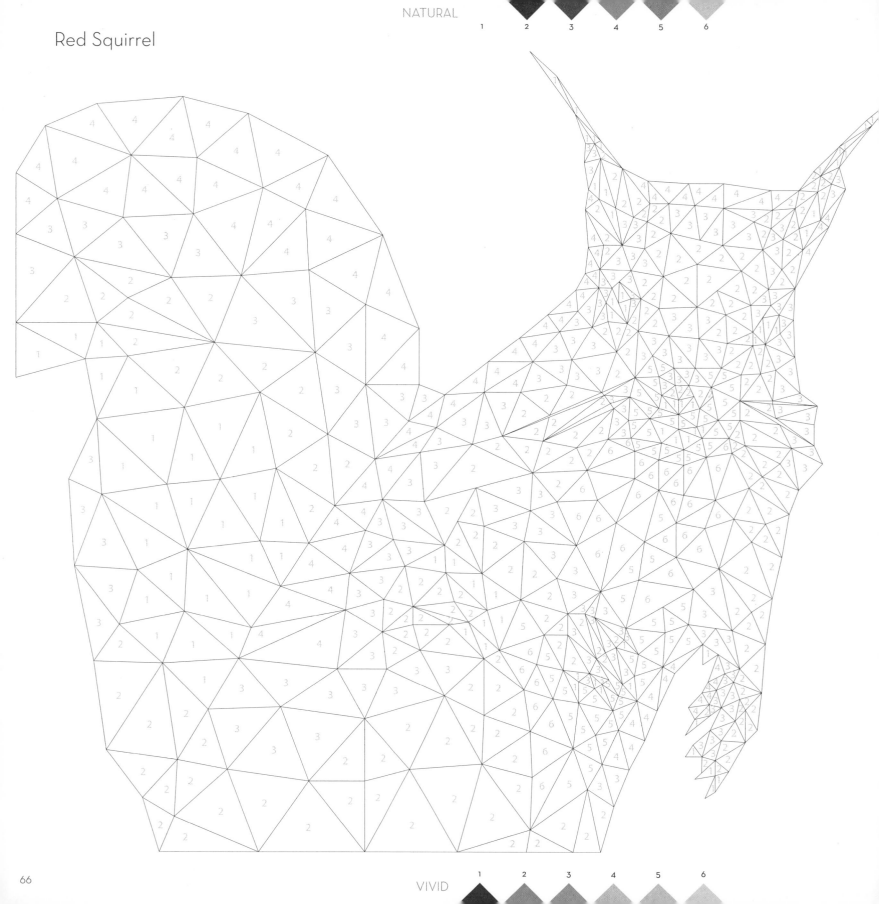

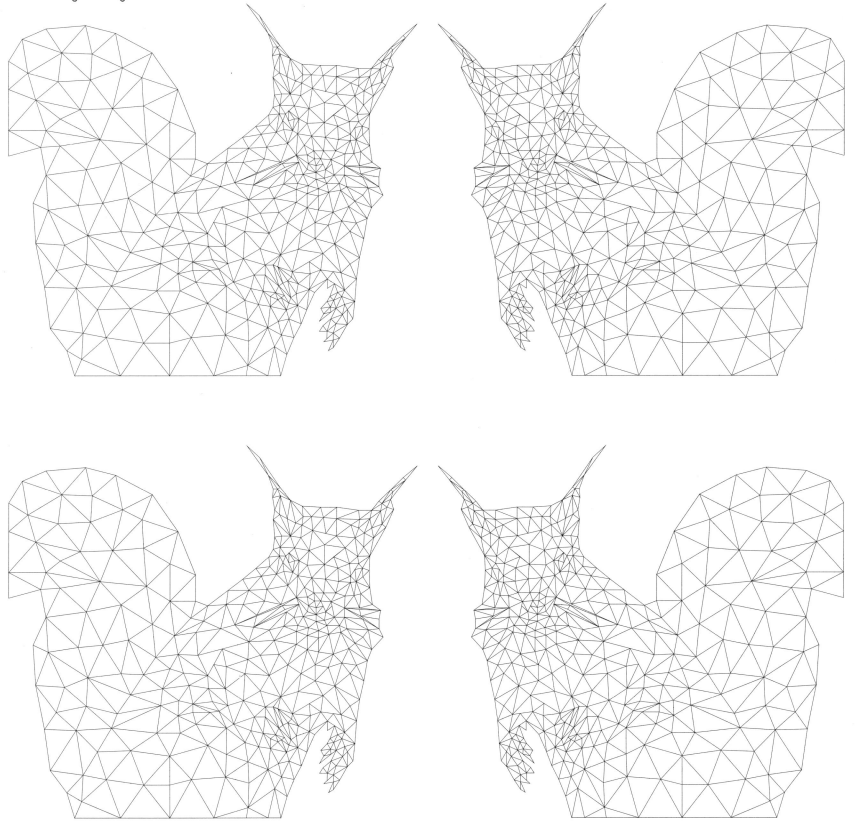

Panda

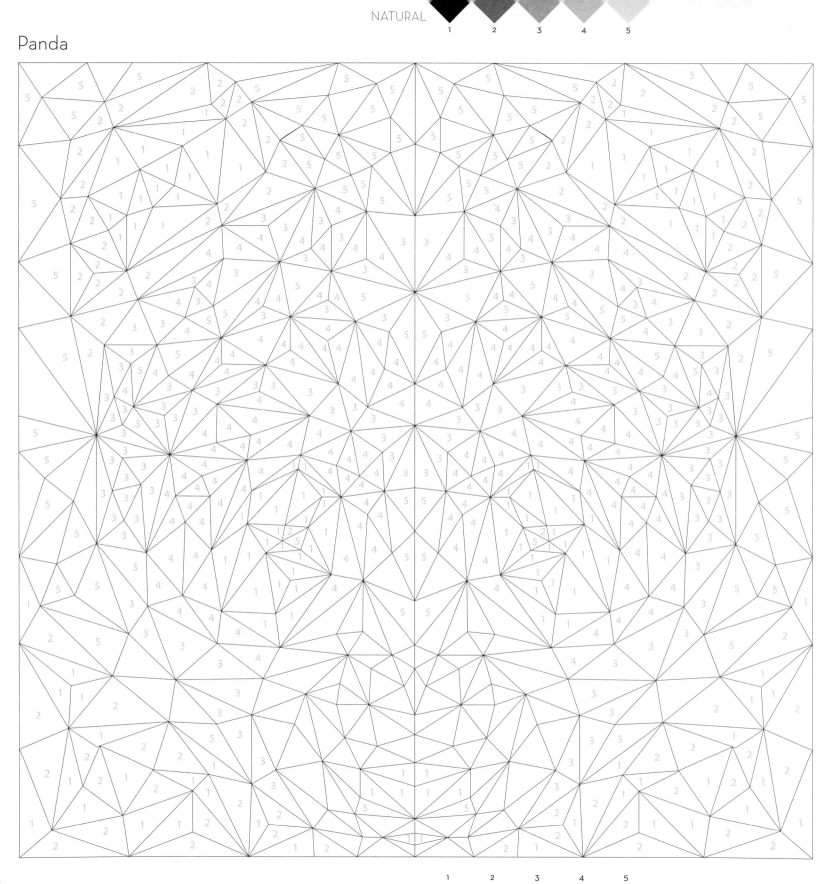

VIVID

Wolf

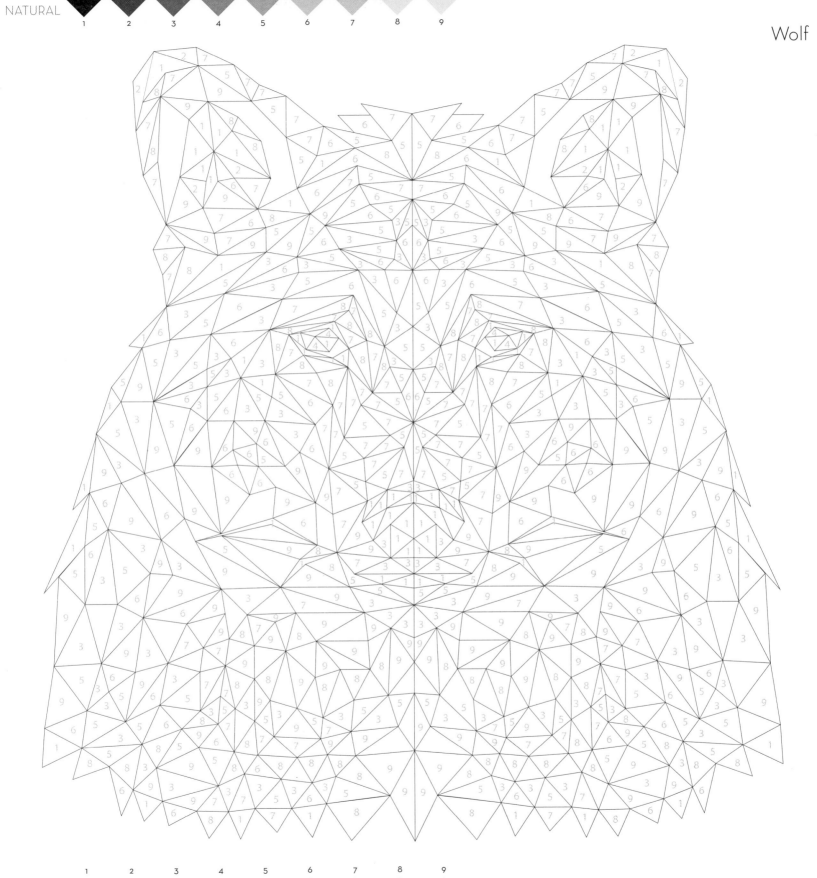

Lioness

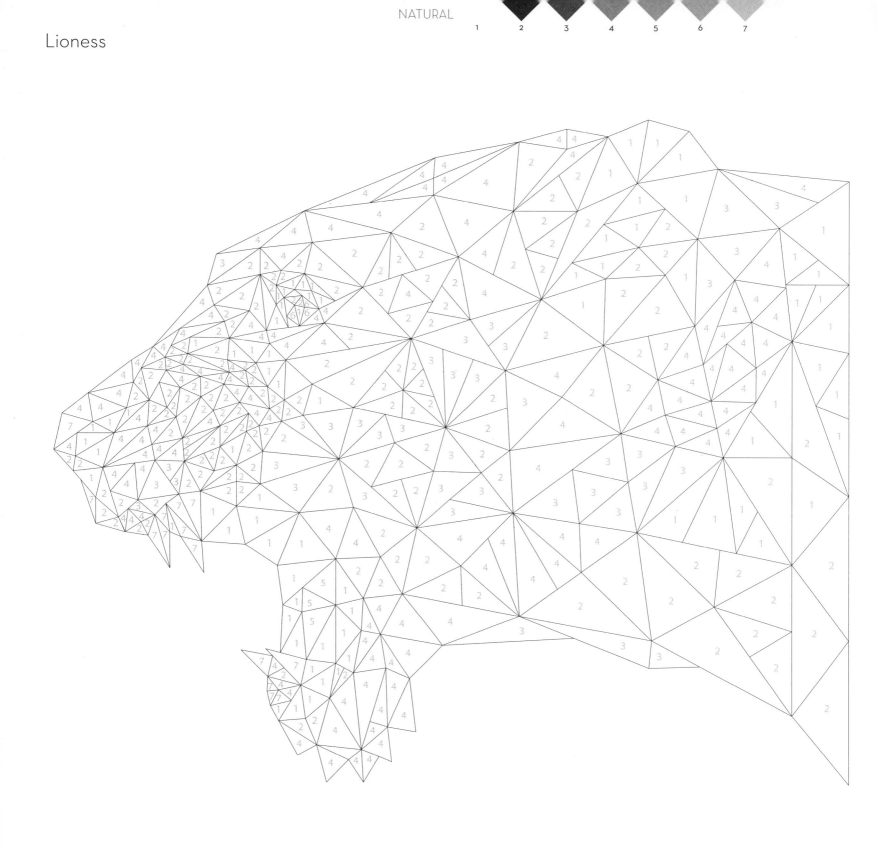

Wombat

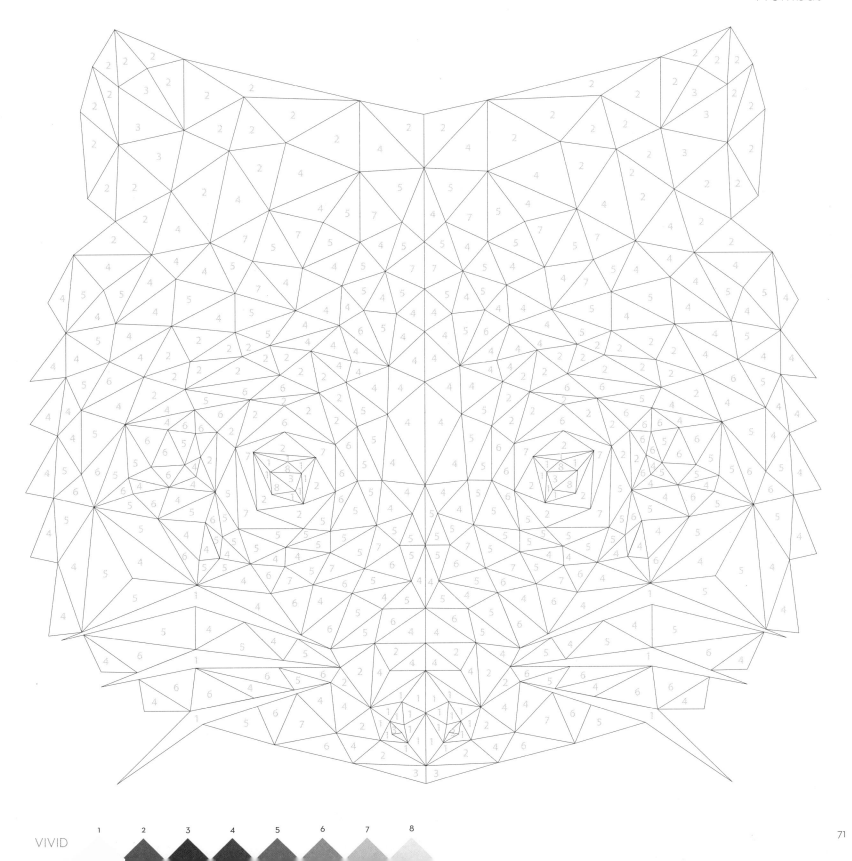

VIVID

Wild Boar

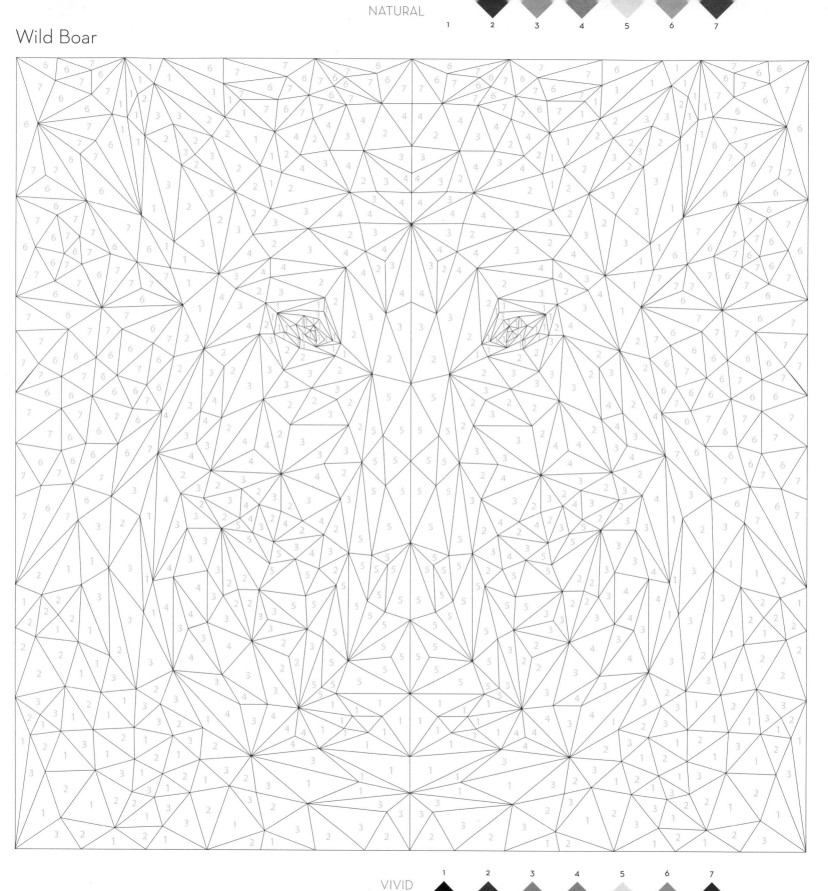

Okapi

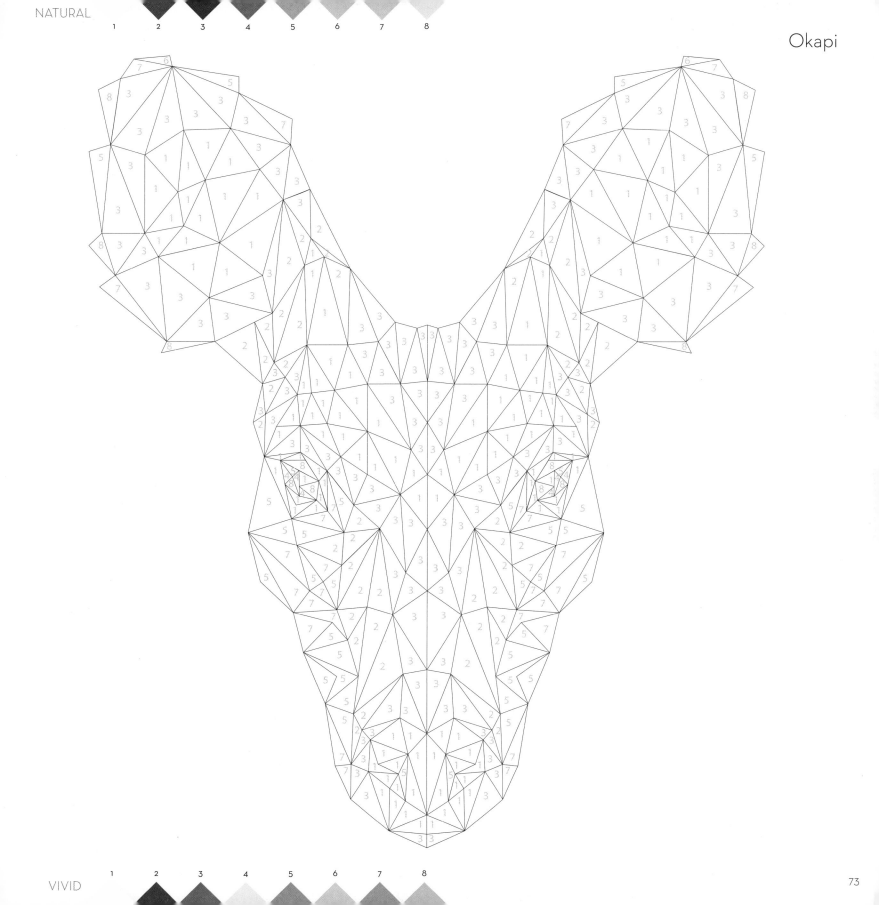

Cape Buffalo

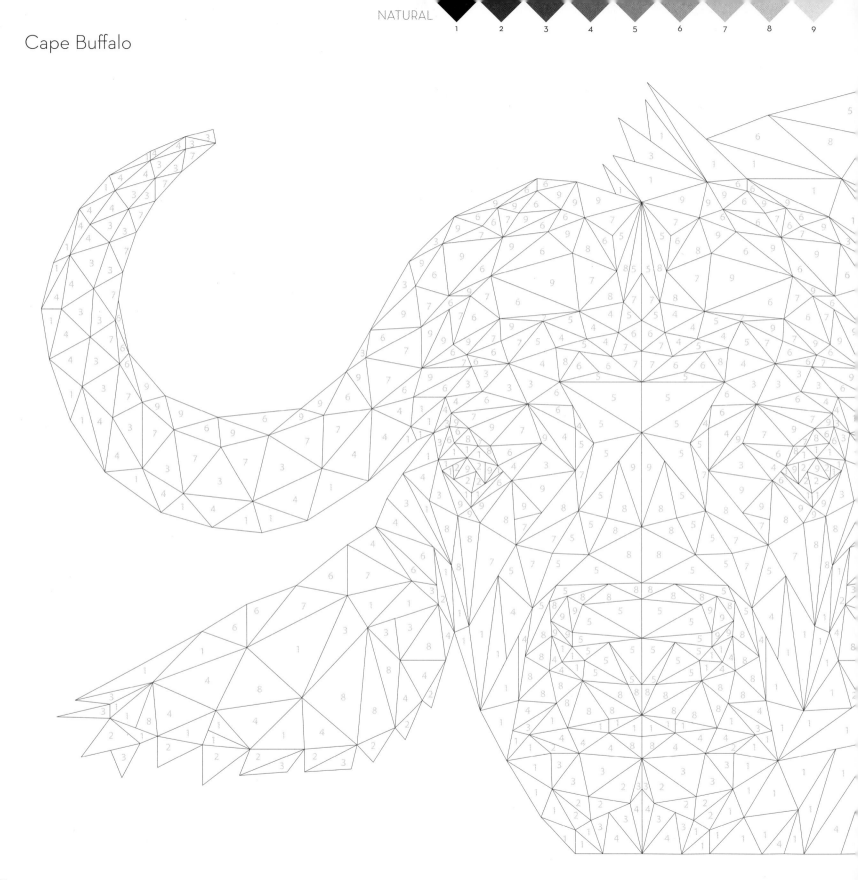

NATURAL   1 2 3 4 5 6 7 8 9

74

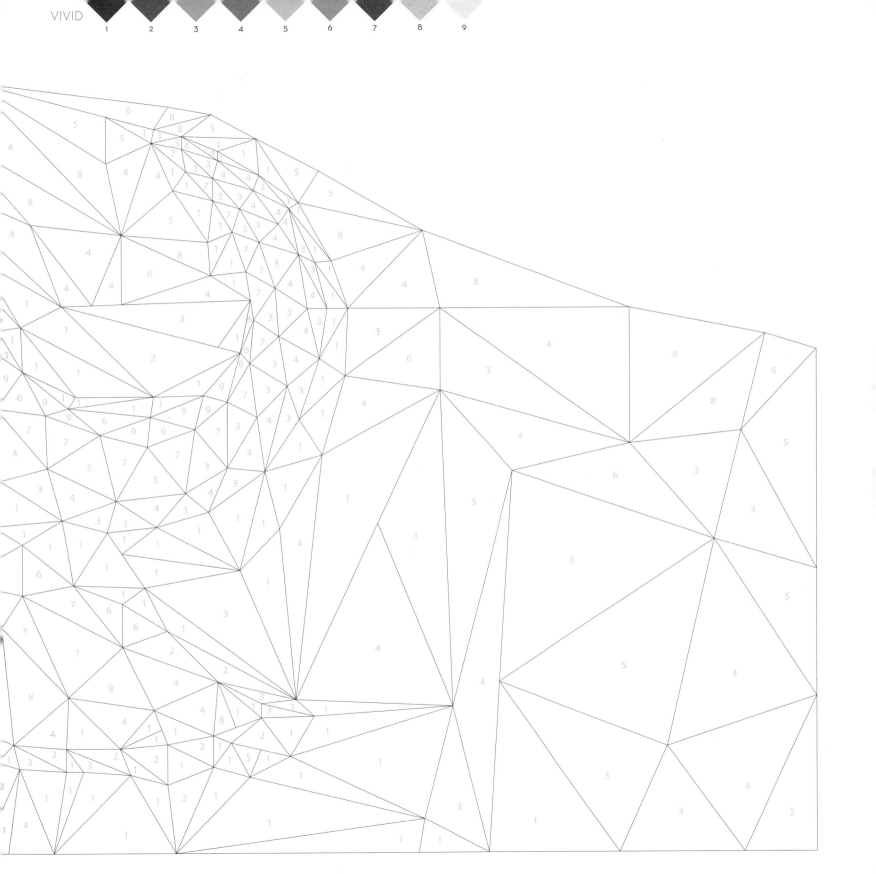

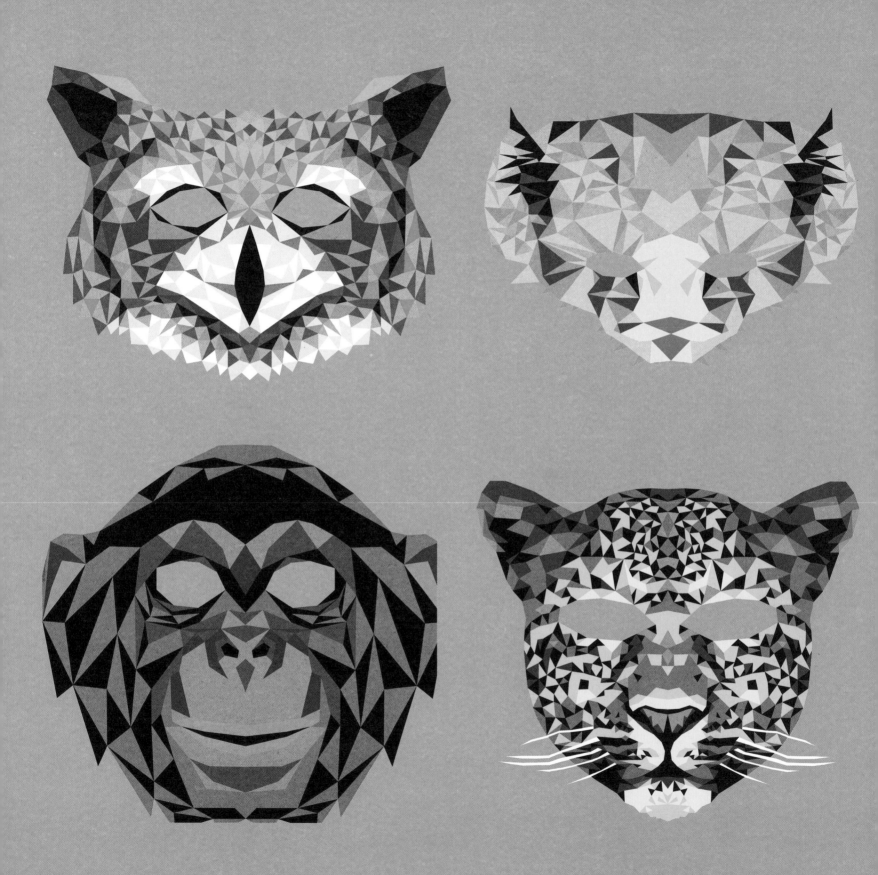

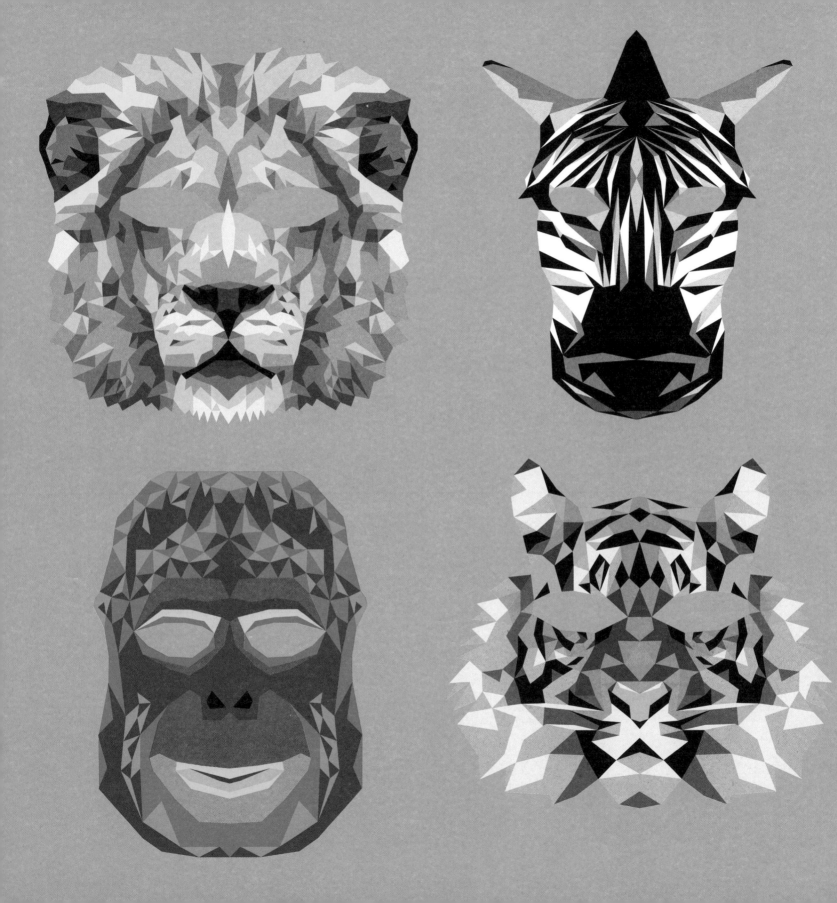

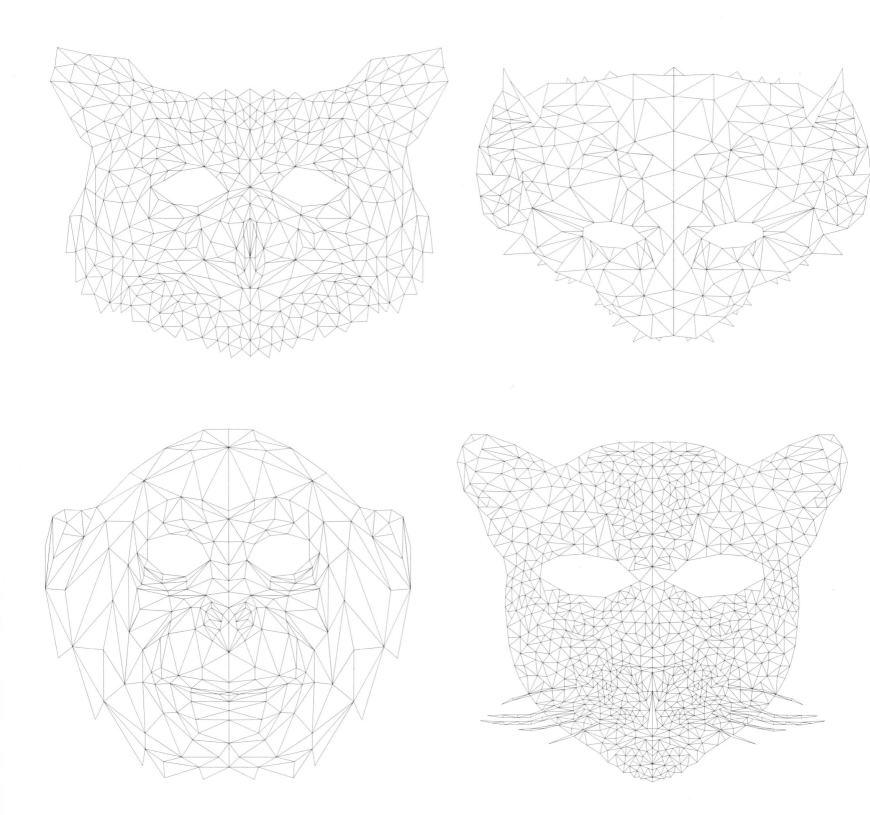

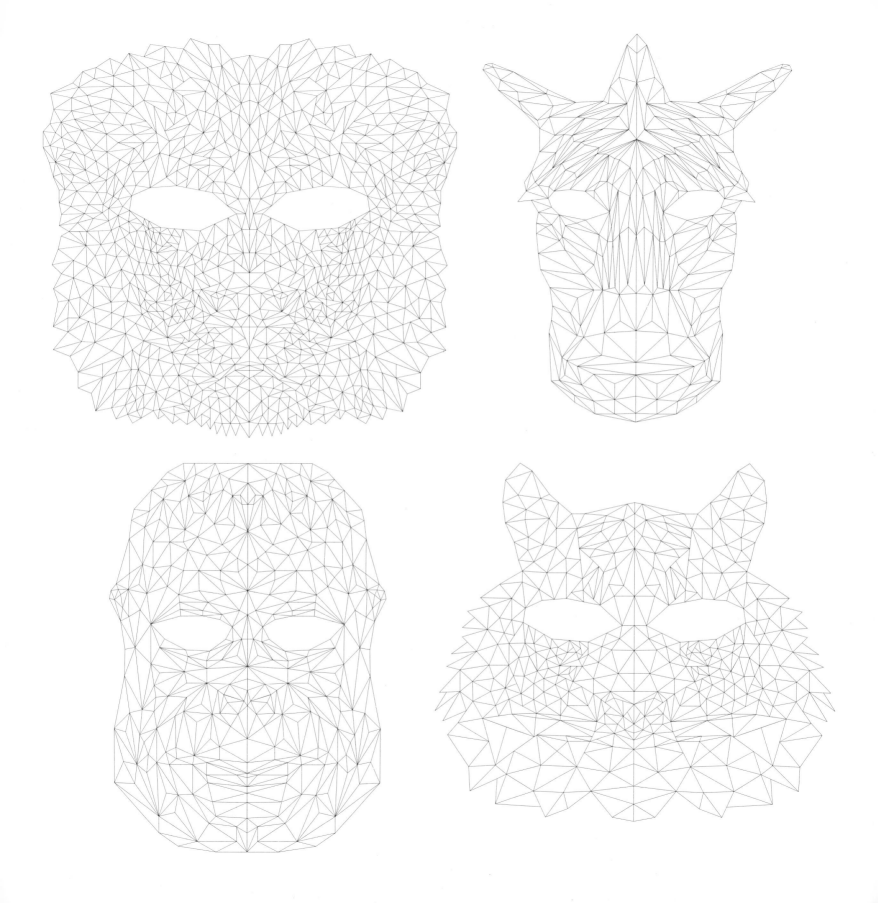

HOW TO MAKE YOUR MASK

Once you have finished coloring your wild animals you may want to use them rather than keep them hidden away in the book. You could frame your finished images and create a whole wall of exotic creatures, adding color to a dreary corner.

For a fun way to show off your works of art, you can also turn your animals into masks. With eight templates to choose from, including a zebra, tiger, owl, and chimpanzee, there's something for everyone. You could do this as a group activity, maybe in your art class, or at work as part of a team-building session.

CREATE YOUR MASK IN THREE EASY STEPS

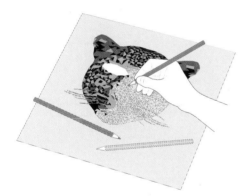

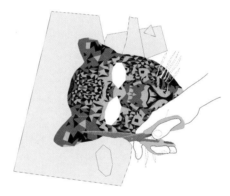

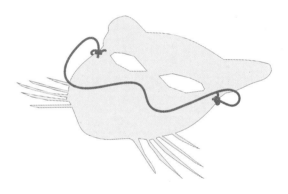

1) Color in your chosen wild animal face using the natural or vivid palette.

2) Carefully tear your finished page out of the book—we've added perforated pages to make this easier. Use scissors or a craft knife to cut around the image and then cut out the two eye shapes. At this stage you may want to reinforce the paper with cardboard for extra stability, but this is not essential.

3) Use a piece of elastic that's suitable for tying at the back of your head to keep the mask in place. Make two small holes on either side of the mask; this is where you will attach the elastic. You can use hole reinforcement stickers (available at craft and stationery stores) so that the elastic doesn't tear your mask. Tie the elastic firmly in place on both sides of the mask. Now you are ready to show off your wild side.

Zebra

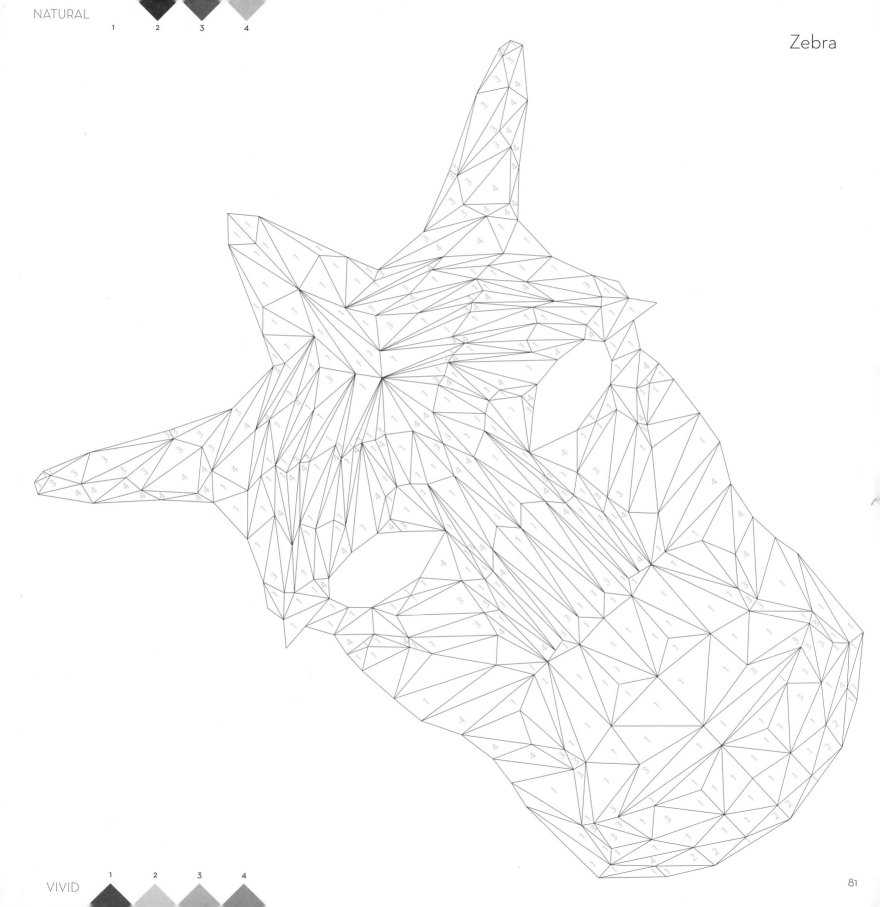

VIVID

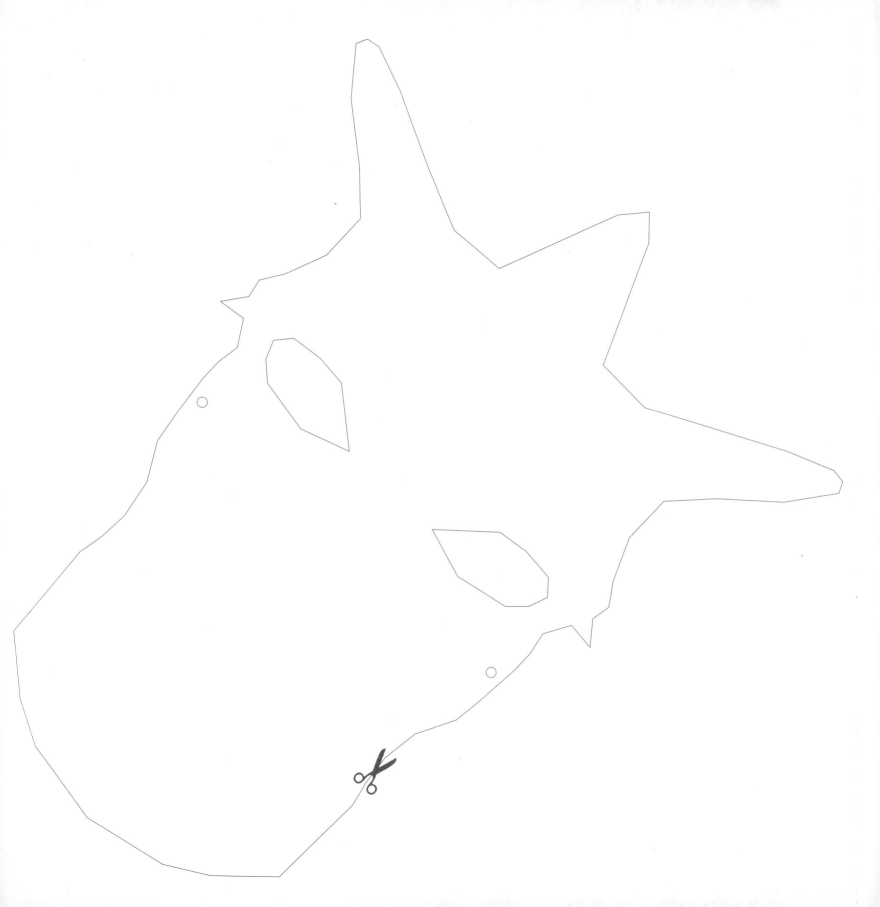

Orangutan

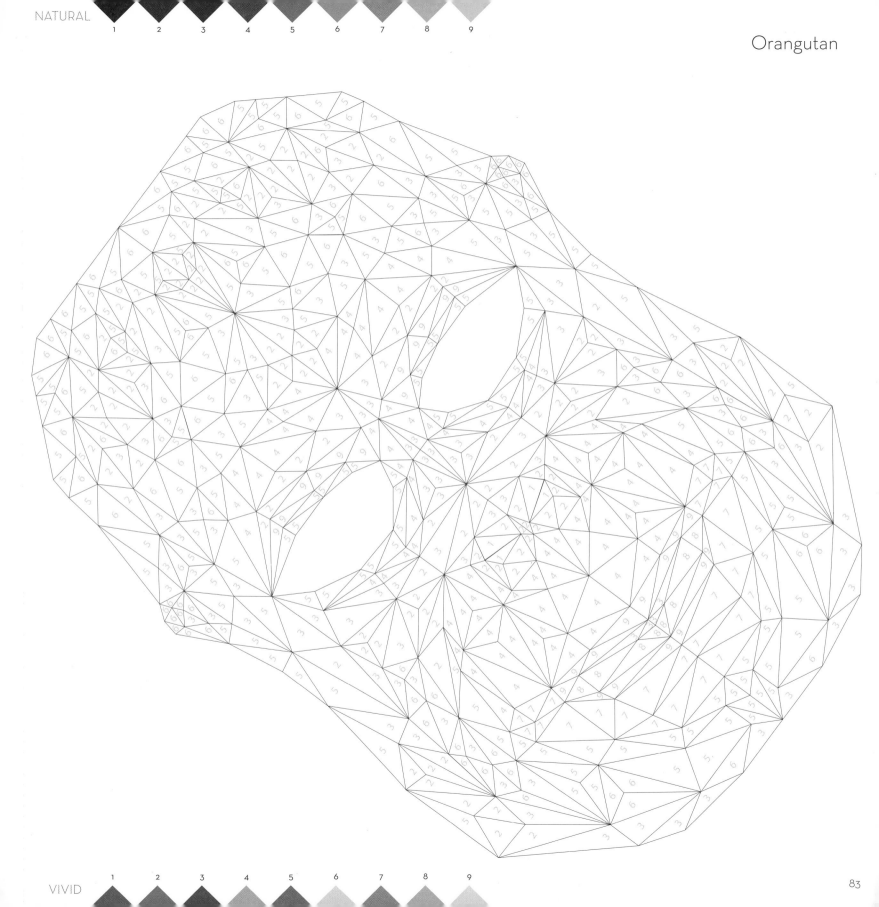

VIVID

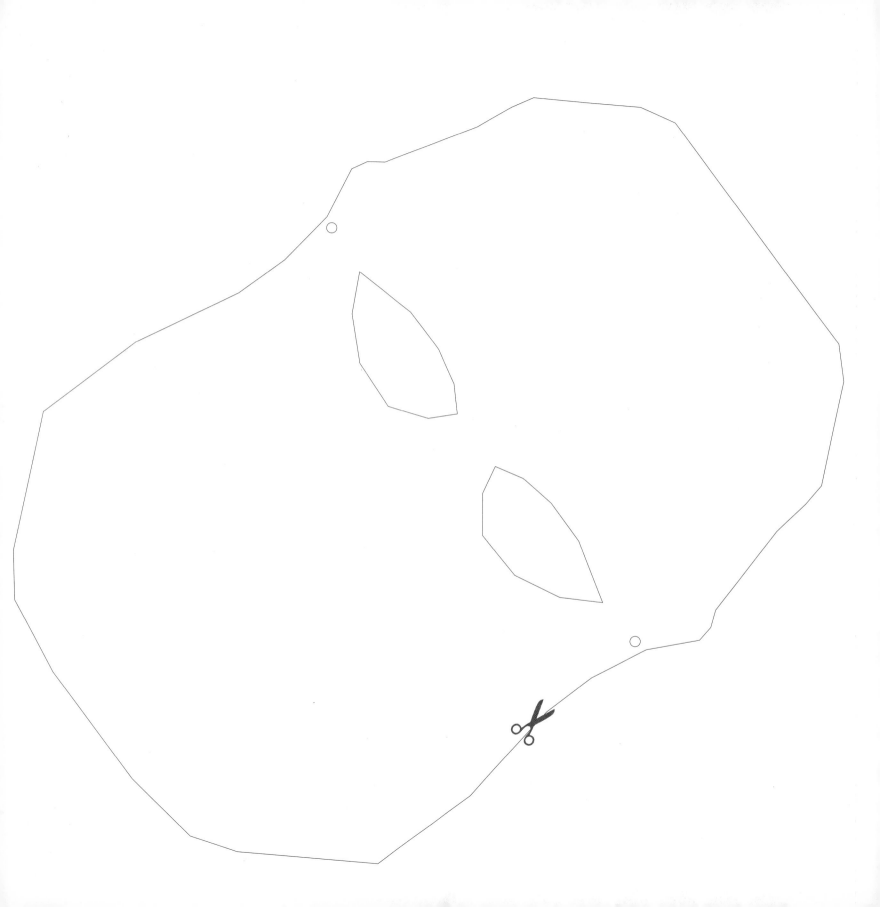

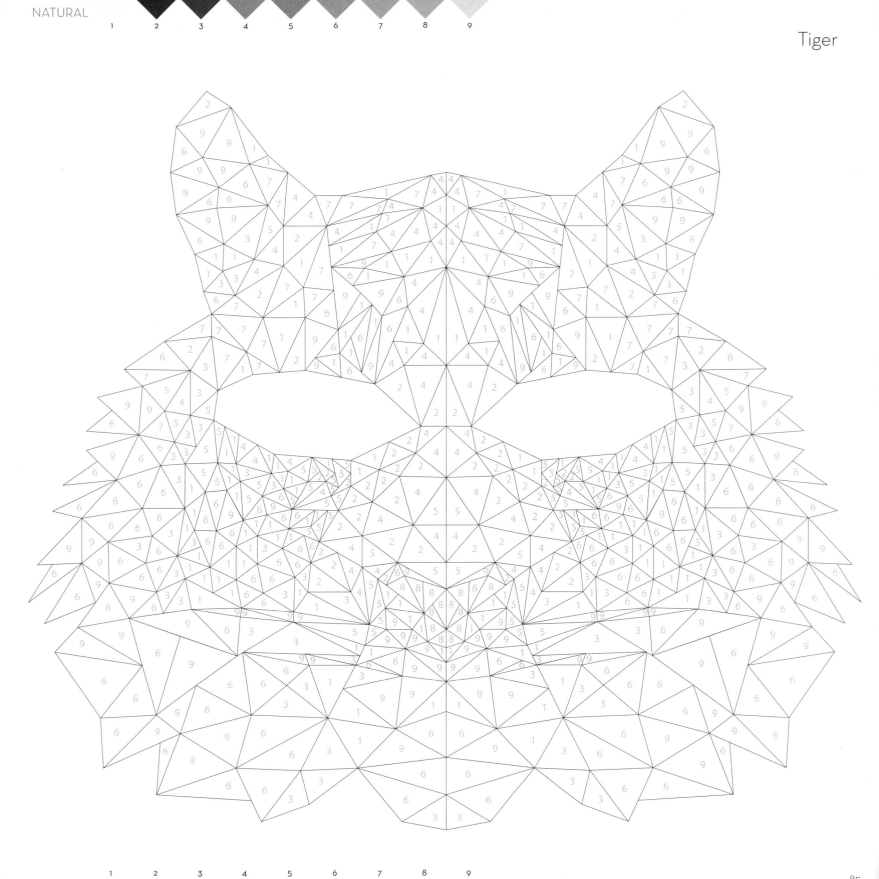

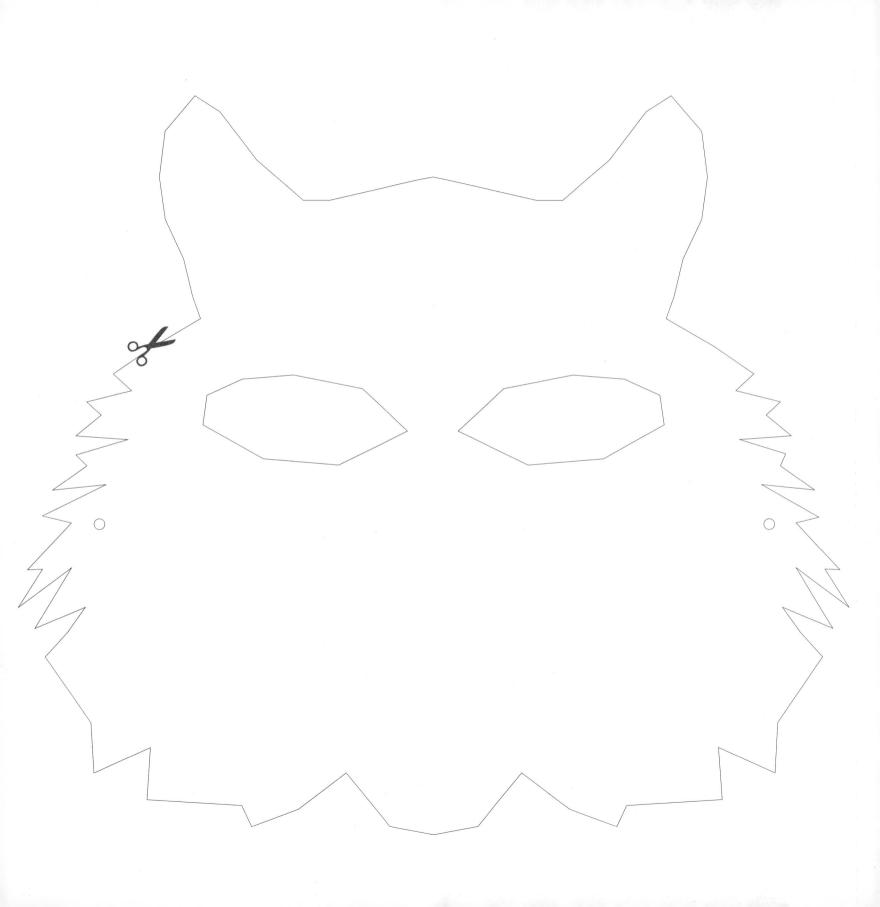

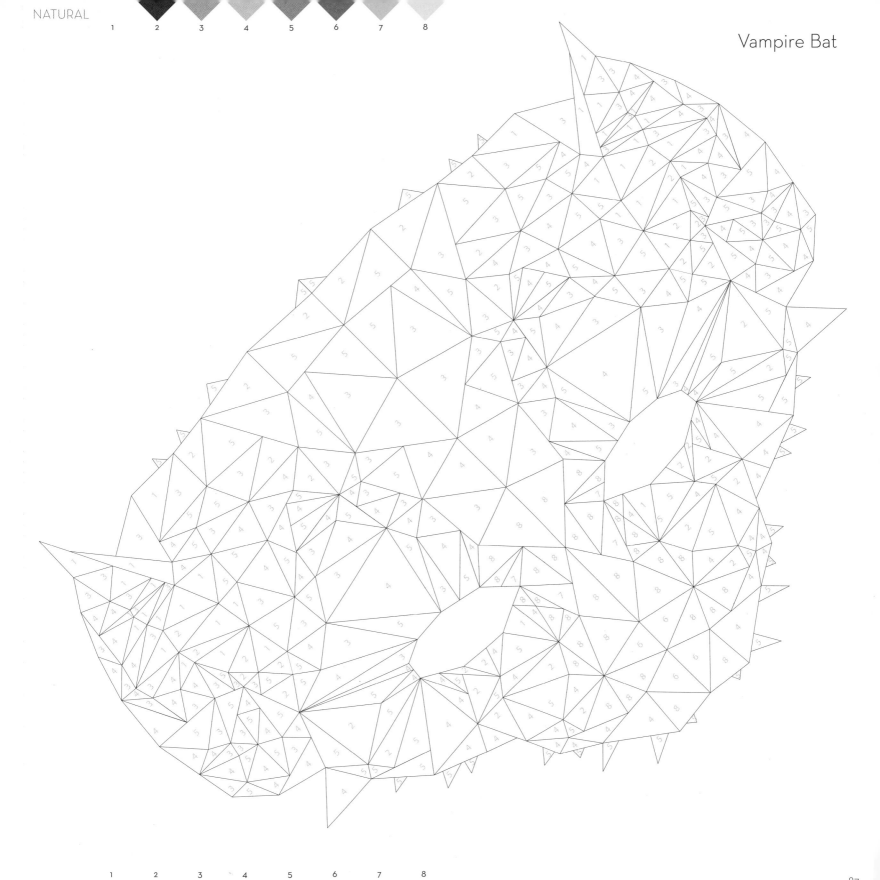

Vampire Bat

VIVID

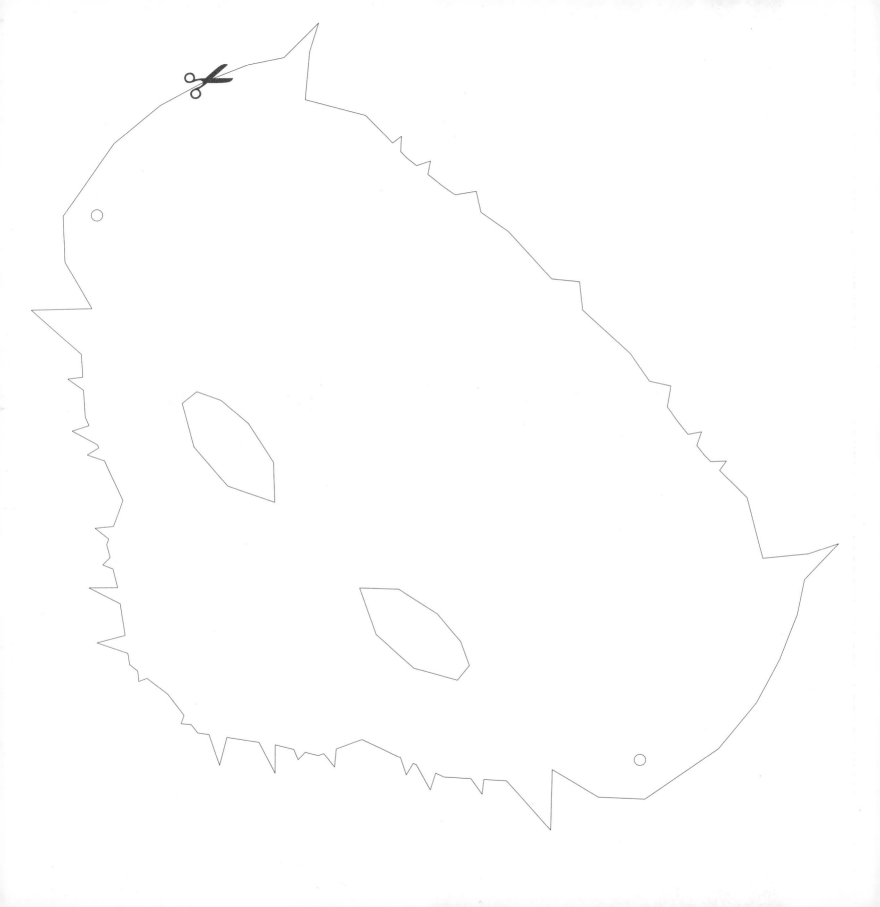

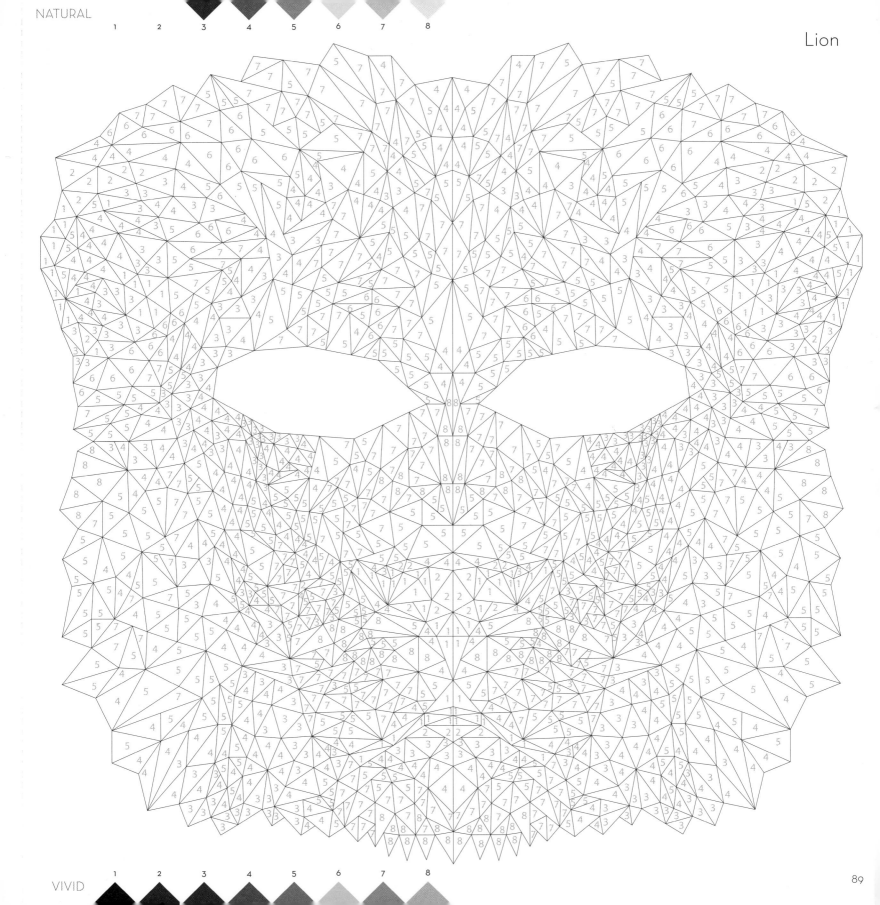

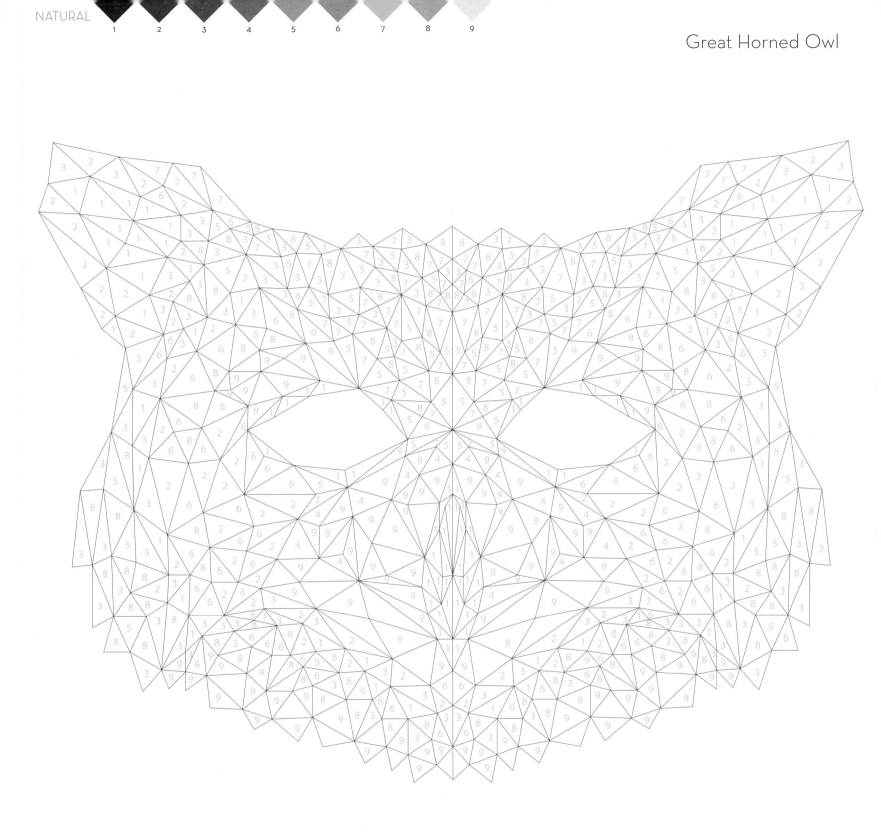

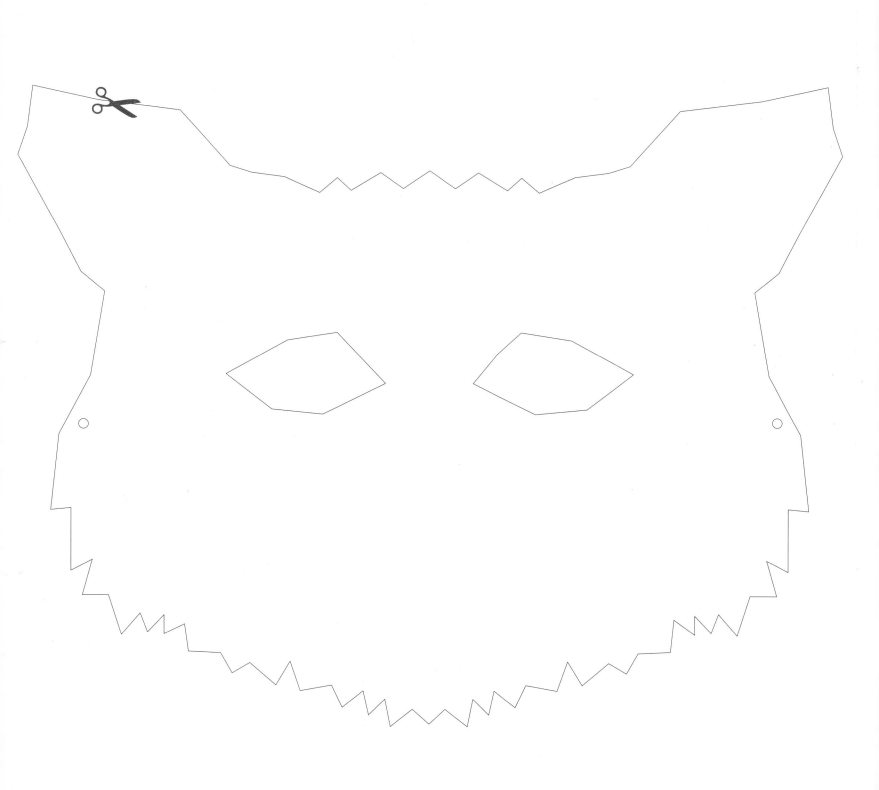

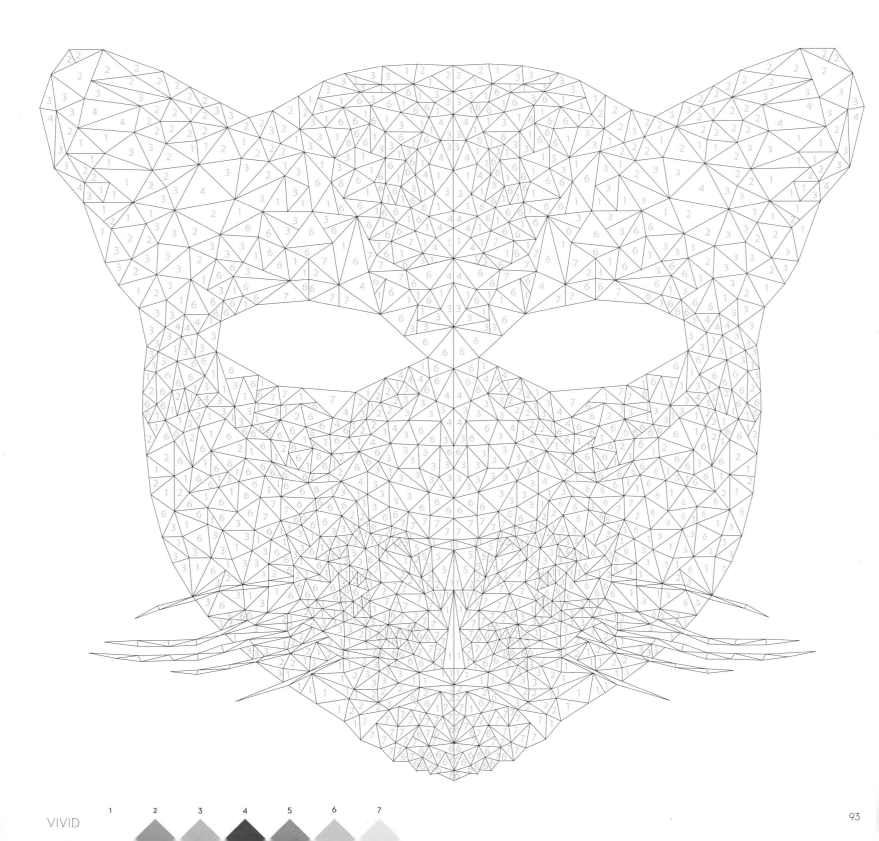

VIVID

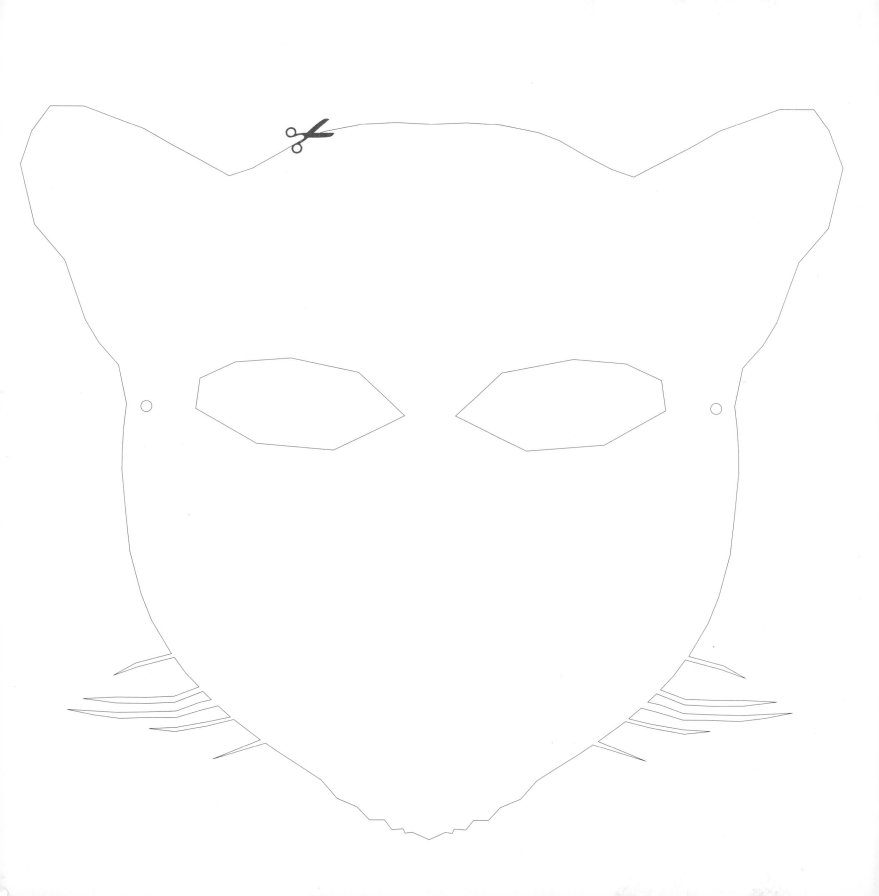

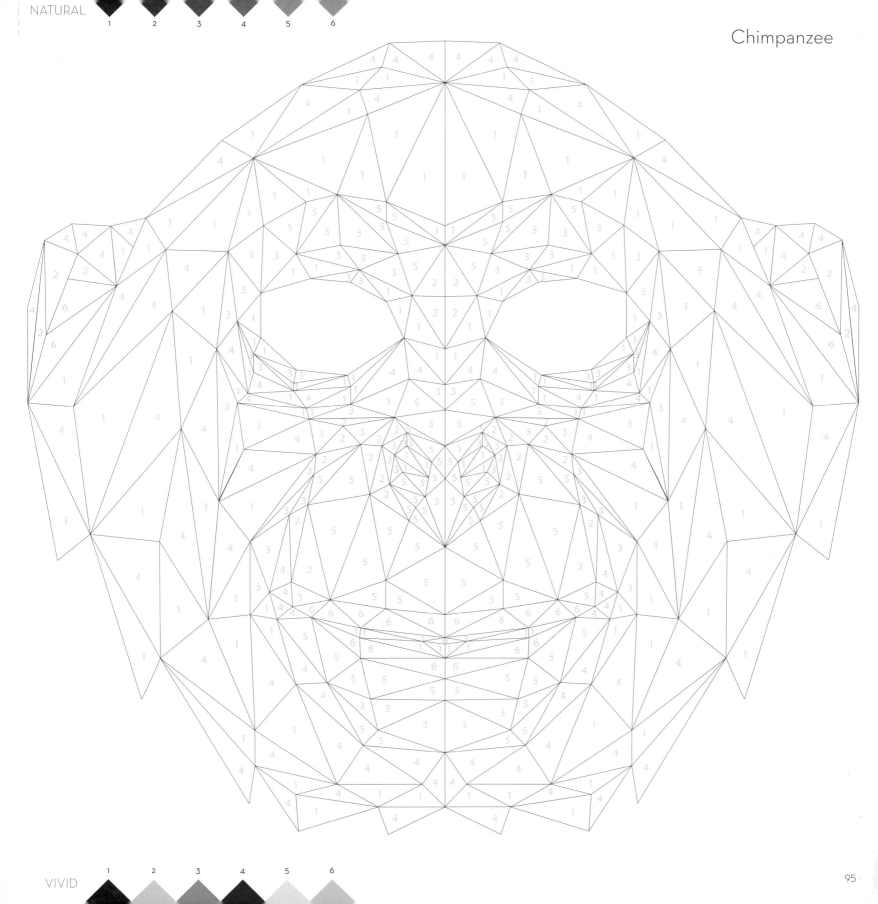

Chimpanzee